SOMETHING
TO
HOLD ONTO

SOMETHING
TO
HOLD ONTO

Autobiographical Sketches

RICHARD COBB

John Murray

First published 1988
by John Murray (Publishers) Ltd
50 Albemarle Street
London W1X 4BD

Typeset in 11/13pt Sabon
at The Spartan Press Ltd
Lymington, Hants
Printed by Mackays of Chatham

Cobb, Richard, 1917–
    Something to hold onto: sketches from a
    Tunbridge Wells childhood.
    1. Kent. Tunbridge Wells. Social life, 1925–1935—
    Childhood reminiscences
    I. Title
    942.2'38

    ISBN 0–7195–4587–0

For
DAISY COBB
born 3 April 1980
and
WILLIAM COBB
born 4 April 1980

Contents

The drawings on pages v, vi, 32, 53 and 168 are by Frank Papé and come from books which he illustrated.

*The Revd Gilbert
Newcomen, a drawing
by Ronald Blythe.*

Introduction

ABOUT THE only thing to be said in favour of *ces événements* of May–June 1968, is that they happened when they did, that is in the middle of the Oxford University term. I was a tutor at the time in Balliol, and my teaching load made it impossible for me to have crossed over to Paris to witness what was going on. Not that, in any case, I would have had any desire to see, even from a prudent distance, the endless and meaningless violence, the uprooted trees, the burning cars, the idiotic graffiti, the posturing, the mountains of filth and rubbish, and to smell the whiff of tear-gas and smouldering rubber. There is something indecent about sitting in on someone else's revolution (not that this disgusting carnival could have been gratified with the dark title of a revolution). I am grateful that I missed out on that episode of French history in action, as portrayed in Thirty-one Tableaux and a hundred side-shows. I would not have enjoyed the sight of the burning books or the flames coming out of the roof of the Sorbonne Library, I would have found it hard to stomach the lying slogans: *maintenant nous sommes tous des juifs allemands*, a triple insult to the Germans, the Jews, and the German Jews, on the part of bored, teen-age, middle-class pseudo-revolutionaries who were French and spoilt and from the *VIIIme* and the *XVIme arrondissements*. I did at least draw a little satisfaction from a member of the Central Committee of the French Communist Party whom, in June, I got to address Balliol JCR, and who called the events of the previous month: *ces enfantillages*. Very nasty childish tricks, indeed.

When I got back to Paris, in July of that year, the mess had been cleared up, the top end of the Boulevard Saint-Michel had been re-tarred, and the would-be revolutionaries had gone off on their summer holidays. One of my former pupils took me on a conducted tour of the *Ecole Normale Supérieure*, rue d'Ulm. The statue to the dead *Normaliens* of two World Wars had been daubed with green paint. But what most caught my attention was a slogan, painted in a sinister black, it seemed from a blow-lamp, repeating, all the way up the *escalier d'honneur*, the question: *Eh bien, Flasselière* (not *Monsieur* Flasselière), *on agonise?* I asked my young friend about this; he told me that M. Flasselière had been the *directeur* of the ENS at the time of the outbreak of the May events, and that, occupying a position of authority, and being in his sixties, he had been the principal butt of the local pseudo-revolutionaries and their allies brought in from outside. He had been insulted to his face—*vieux con*, and that sort of thing—had been spat upon, his study had been broken into and wrecked, and he had suffered a heart attack. I think he was still alive at the time of my visit, but it is possible that the wish so liberally and coyly expressed on the walls may have been gratified shortly afterwards.

My friend, Jean Lequillier, who had been *Vice-Recteur* of Nanterre, a position even more exposed, had been shut out of his office, reviled, and physically assaulted, over a period of several weeks. He, too, had had a heart attack. In the following autumn he had been appointed *Directeur* of the *Maison Française d'Oxford*, a quiet haven that he very much appreciated, and a position that he only occupied for less than a year, dying of a massive heart attack in his official residence. I don't know if the Nanterre students knew of his death. I imagine it would have given them a great deal of satisfaction.

My friend Jean Vidalenc, Professor of History at the University of Rouen, had ha the door of his office kicked in, his papers scattered and thrown out of the window, his face slapped, and had been subjected to the statutory torrent of abuse from this student action group, led by a junior lecturer who had recently been appointed by the Professor. This Jean, too, had had a heart attack in the course of the summer. He died of a massive heart attack sixteen years later. I think the Mont Saint-Aignan students may have hastened that outcome.

Some of the French friends of Mavis Gallant, whose diary of May–June 1968, has recently been published, took to reading up the history of the Commune, in between tours of duty on the barricades. They must have been disappointed that, despite the barricades, there had (apparently) been no corpses in the street (and, no corpses in the street, no Revolution). But certainly any number of people in their fifties and sixties must have been put at risk.

What was their crime in the eyes of the *apprentis-Saint-Justs* of the *XVIme*? To have been what they were: fifty year olds, sixty year olds, *vieux cons, croulants*, or whatever other amiable collective name was given to them. This was a new form of totalitarianism: the exclusion, and, preferably, the elimination, of a whole age group, of several age groups. The old were irredeemable, they represented a new form of 'class enemies', and, like 'class enemies', they were destined for the scrap-heap. The redeemed, the only redeemable, were confined to those in their teens, their twenties, and, *à la rigueur*, their early thirties. All monopolies of virtue are terrifying, but what could be more terrifying than the monopoly of the young? What is the merit of just being young? Or, for that matter, of just being *any* age? *On a l'âge que l'on a. Not* a slogan of May 1968.

Nothing about the dreadful *soixante-huitards* – now, mostly, I suppose, in their forties – shocked me more than this lack of respect for, more, this active hatred of, the old. This has nothing to do with my present age. I have never been especially aware of my own age at any given time in my life: 'Where should I be now that I am forty-five?' and that sort of preoccupation. I think that on the whole I have been able to live very happily quite outside the conscious awareness of age groups (having a son approaching eight helps in that respect.) But, ever since my childhood, I have enjoyed the company of those much older than myself. I sought them out because they knew so much more than I did, had lived so much longer, had memories extending back far into the previous century. Of course, I have been singularly fortunate, both in my grandparents, my uncles (on both sides), my mother, my father (whom I knew so little and who, over the gap of more than fifty years, I am endeavouring to get to know better), and my sister's in-laws. Add to these a great many of my French friends – a sadly diminishing band – among my elders. Perhaps one can write better about those one detests: a hated mother, a much-loathed father, may be the starting-off point of a literary vocation. Hervé Bazin had to take to writing in order to get his mother, the frightful *Folcoche*, out of his system. Once he had

3

written *Folcoche* out of his system – it took him two books to finish
her off – his novels started to peter out. Be this as it may, in this
present chronicle of elders and betters, the connecting link is
affection, gratitude, and enlightenment. Most of those who form the
subject of the book were indeed both older and better than me. But
their place is far from exclusive. Many of those who figure in my
itineraries, from Irène onwards, were children, some again were my
contemporaries, or were younger than myself. In nearly thirty-five
years of university teaching, much of it in tutorials – one to one, or
with a pair – I have been very lucky in my pupils: almost all have been
pleasant, sociable, polite, without being fulsome, very easy to get on
with, some of them very intelligent and imaginative, many of them as
innately frivolous as their tutor – I have never been very much aware
of the so-called 'generation gap'; indeed, I think it is a product either
of fiction or, worse, of sociology. I have not been able to make any
clear distinction between my pupils of the sixties, and those of the
seventies and the eighties. They have all seemed very much the same.
Perhaps I have missed out on the importance of decades. Certainly, as
far as I know, none of my pupils has actively looked forward to my
departure from this world. If any had, he or she would have been
discreet enough not to have advertised publicly his or her private
hopes for my early demise. Indeed, I have derived as much happiness
from the frequentation of the young and the very young, as from the
old and the very old, for they point the way towards an unchartable
future, and they offer, if not the guarantee, at least the promise, like
well used itineraries, of continuity. But, old, or young, close, or
observed from a distance, I cannot separate them from their physical
environment, whether on the move, or at rest: Frank Papé in the dark
dining-room; my mother sitting just inside the large French bay
windows facing onto the wrought-iron balcony of 5 A; my uncle
Primus striding along Clacton Pier, his watch in his hand, swinging
his stick; my Uncles Jack and Vernon, with their hats on indoors; my
grandmother, wearing a veil, sitting in the shade in her part of the
garden; my grandfather, with a panama on his head and long
buttoned-up black boots on his feet, sunning himself on a garden
bench, with Tim-Tom on his lap; the old lady in the strange black
round hat, out on her rocking-chair, on the porch of her wooden

house, down near the railroad tracks, in Columbia, South Carolina; my old friend, Jean Meuvret, walking with majestic slowness, talking all the time, and, every now and then, seizing me by the lapel, and turning on himself, and turning me round too, down the rue des Archives. So my book is as much a plea for regularity, the firmest guarantee of reassurance, as for affection. I am a poor hater, my hatreds have never been consistent, swivelling round, in quite short periods, like a mad barometer; I seem to have been much more reliable on affections. But I am still an enquiring, attentive walker. Even in my own itineraries, I remain an onlooker, an observer. I think I have always endeavoured to keep away from the centre of things. That is why I claim to be a provincial.

As on so many previous occasions – three or four at least – I have to express my affectionate and grateful thanks to my sister, Diana, my elder by seven years, and my better by a lifetime, and who has given me an enormous amount of help, both on the subject of her father-in-law, Frank Papé, and on that of Uncle Vernon, whom she was old enough to have known as a generous and attentive host at the dinner parties that he was in the habit of giving, at his house in Glebe Place, in the early and mid 1930s, at a time when I was still a schoolboy. Her memory going back seven years further than mine, to reach even to the far side of the great divide of the summer of 1914, she has also been able to provide me with details about my father's career in Somaliland and in the Sudan, her own early childhood at her Aunt Mabel's, in Bessels House, Bessels Green, near Sevenoaks, our other aunts, our uncles, our grandparents, our cousin Daisy, our cousin Roland Swindale, her exact contemporary and the son of our Uncle Jack, and our cousins, Kenneth and Marjorie Cobb, the children of my father's middle brother, Uncle Arthur. Thanks to Diana, too, I have been able to re-establish the succession of our nannies, from Rose to our own shared Kate, and to list at least some of the scores of houses in which we lived, at one time or another, first in Frinton, then in Tunbridge Wells.

My first cousin, Marjorie Beggs, née Cobb, was most helpful, while on a recent visit from her home in British Columbia, in providing me with information about her parents' venture with the boarding-house in Folkestone, after her father had given up his work in the Southwold brewery. She also explained to me why we had never met as children at St Leonard's House. She filled me in with the details of her own career. My cousin John was equally informative about his father's career, Marjorie's brother, Kenneth.

My brother-in-law – he has been that for more than fifty years – Lionel Papé, and my nephew, Barry Papé, have been patient in answering my many queries on the subject of their father and grandfather, Frank C. Papé, the artist and book-illustrator, and one of the three residents of Percy House, Tunbridge Wells. Barry was able to provide me with a comprehensive list of all his grandfather's published works. Lionel supplied me with details about Newlands, the preparatory school at Seaford which he attended for seven years and at which his mother taught for twenty or thirty years. Further information on the subject of Seaford prep schools between the wars and since the Second World War has been provided by my old school friend – we were in the History Side at Shrewbury together – Arthur Pyper, for many years the headmaster of a prep school of his own. For anyone seeking further information on the subject of Seaford as the principal capital of prep-school-land, both during the war and the ten years that followed it, I would recommend Jeremy Lewis's marvellously funny autobiography, *Playing for Time*, published last year.

The essay, 'The House in the Hythe', first appeared in a collection, entitled *Places*, published in 1980, by the Oxford University Press, for Oxfam, and edited by the Suffolk writer, Ronald Blythe. It was thanks to this entirely happy experience of co-operation that I first came into regular contact with the author of *Akenfield*, who now lives just outside Colchester, having moved across into Essex. In the last seven years Ronnie has provided me with a wealth of information concerning St Leonard's Church, once a Balliol living, and closed since 1983, and its one-time incumbents, the vicar, Canon Henry Carter, and his assistant, the Revd Gilbert Newcomen. Ronnie first met the latter when he was seventeen and when the Revd Newcomen was close on ninety. The same generous informant was able to provide me not only with a photograph, c. 1930, of the two 'Divines', but also with his own sketch of the Revd Newcomen, wearing a shovel hat and a sort of *soutane*, and carrying a string bag containing his shopping.

The Colchester painter, John Bensusan-Butt, the nephew and pupil of Lucien Pissarro, has provided me not only with the surveyor's plan of St Leonard's House, shortly before its demolition sometime in the 1950s, but also with the details of the Revd Newcomen's funeral, in August 1952, the list of mourners – there were not many of them, he had outlived by many years most of his contemporaries – and the sale of his effects. It was also from him that I learnt that his mother, Dr Ruth Bensusan-Butt, had qualified as a doctor in 1910, putting up her plate the same year. From about that time, till the death of 'Mrs Ma' late in 1926, she had been my grandmother's doctor. The letter in which he gave me these and other details – the doctor had been a leading figure in the campaign for women's suffrage – of his mother's career sparked off in my memory, over a period of well over sixty years, a very faint, yet precise, echo. Yes, I could indeed recall, now that he had mentioned it, that curiously trinitarian surname –at the age of six, I had at one time thought that it must have referred to three people, two male, one female – coming up in conversations between my grandparents over the lunchtable. Not that the doctor's services can often have been called on down in the Hythe, my grandmother's health having remained extremely good well on into her late-eighties. The reminder of the doctor's surname was rather like the return of a very old friend, after a long absence. I am extremely grateful to John Bensusan-Butt for having thus all at once provided me with an unexpected link with a distant and blissfully happy childhood in the Hythe. So I have been especially fortunate in my two Colchester informants, the one, Ronnie Blythe, an emigrant from Suffolk, the other, a 'Colchester native' of several generations, whose beautiful Georgian family house in the Minories is now the municipal museum.

I would like to thank the Tunbridge Wells Civic Society for having invited me to give a public talk in the lecture room of the Museum and Public Library. The subject of my talk, which provides the opening passage of the chapter on Percy House, was the old Public Library.

My affectionate thanks for having put up with me for so many years go to my old friends of Rookley days, Jim and Nancy Mennell, now my neighbours here in Wolvercote, so that they still have to put up with me

– a risk that they took when they made the move from Tunbridge Wells – though no longer every night of the week.

Thanks are due to Mrs H. J. C. Warren, of Worthing, a direct descendant of Martha Cobb, of Copford, my grandfather's sister, for having provided me with a photocopy of the will of Nathaniel Cobb, drawn up in 1830, and with details of the Cobb family tree. I would also like to thank the Secretary of Girton College, Cambridge, for having sent me so promptly the dates at which my Aunt Mabel (Mabel Swindale, 1893–1897) had been an undergraduate at the College, and those at which my Aunt Jane (Jane Swindale, 1921–1932) had carried out the functions of Garden Steward there.

My debts to my friend and former Balliol pupil, Roger Butler, are once more considerable. Having previously tried out on him the first drafts of various sections of *Still Life* and of *A Classical Education*, I have once more taken advantage of his good nature by renewing the process, with a number of readings from the present book. As always, his comments have been pertinent and his criticisms have been of much profit to me. If my books have gained in readability and in concision in the process, it is to a very large extent due to Roger. It is the mark of a true friend never to be sparing of criticisms.

Editors are of quite vital importance to authors; at least, that has been very much my experience over the years. I have always liked to feel that, when writing, I was addressing myself to my editor, and to him alone. It is a feeling that humanises, personalises, the actual process of writing. It is even better when the editor is also a friend. This is the third book I have written for Hugo Brunner, and I hope that there will be several more. I have followed Hugo from Chatto & Windus to John Murray. I would willingly follow him anywhere.

In May last year, I reached the age of seventy. In the preceding April, William reached that of seven. I make no bold claims on the future, that would not be wise. But I like to think that, at some later date, William may read this book. It would tell him how lucky his father has been, not only in his elders and betters, but also in his contemporaries and in his pupils.

Wolvercote, January, 1988.

ONE

Itineraries

HERE THEN are the two little photos. In the one, I am bending right down, almost double, half hidden in the blackberry bush, my face in profile, a branch of my spectacles showing. In the other, I am seen from the front, advancing well into the bush, holding up a little basket, the sort that had once contained raspberries, one cannot see the blackberries. In both I am wearing a black trilby, bought earlier that year from Berteil, Boulevard Saint-Germain, and a heavy mackintosh – in an effort to defy the late-summer heat – with the buttons hidden. Both the black hat and the mac, as well as the wide-knotted French tie, if it could be seen, are designed to emphasize my civilian status; the hat has the secondary and quite unrealizable purpose of making me look middle-aged. I am probably also wearing a dark three-piece suit, made by an elderly tailor in Monson Road, and, although the photo does not show my feet, grey spats, in a further effort to escape from my twenty-third year. The hat hides most of my face, so that only my sharp nose and my round horn-rimmed glasses are visible beneath the black brim. I am certainly *trying* to look middle-aged. I am rather more successful with a civilian appearance so triumphantly vaunted. We are about a fortnight into the Second World War, Poland must be pretty nearly finished by now, though Warsaw and Westeplatte are still holding out. Tunbridge Wells has not been bombed as yet. I am not carrying, as I should be, my little box-like gasmask.

Blackberrying somewhere up beyond the Cemetery, on the far side of Forest Road, and a bit past the Golf Course (a steady supplier to the Cemetery), as well as being a normal early- or mid-September activity, has been chosen, that afternoon, in a timid, perhaps rather pathetic effort to underline the continuity between a state of peace and the new and terrible state of war; certainly this is how I, at least, would have seen it, in my overriding anxiety to keep the awful events far away in the East at a safe distance from the Kent and Sussex border. At this time of the year – blackberrying season – we would probably have been similarly engaged in 1936, 1937, and 1938; and I for one would be making a tentative claim on the future: we would be back here, among the same bushes, off the steep road leading down towards the little ford, the well and the duck-pond, in 1940.

I don't think my three companions were quite as much aware of the inner significance of our activities as I was at the time. Two of them, Nancy and Brigid, were girls of my age who were not yet directly affected by the outbreak of hostilities. For them it would have been blackberrying just for the sake of it. The third, Jim, a very large man in a blazer, rather older – I think he must have been in his late-twenties – did not take part in the blackberrying and sat quietly in the back seat of the big car. He was still recovering from a bad bout of rheumatic fever; his father, a well-known Harley Street consultant, had given strict orders that he was not to over-exert himself. 1939 was rather a good time to have rheumatic fever; it looked very much as if he would not have to worry at all about the war. Not that I was in any imminent danger, either; I had come back from Paris in late-July feeling very ill indeed. The X-Rays had revealed a spot on my right lung. I was living at home and was being treated for pleurisy – I can no longer remember what the treatment consisted of, though I do recall that heat applied to the right side of my back afforded me some comfort – as an outpatient at the Kent & Sussex Hospital. Pleurisy was perhaps not quite such a trump card as Jim's rheumatic fever; still, I had been rather lucky in my timing, and my precious civilian status – to which I dressed so assiduously – did not seem to be immediately threatened, the spot would not go away in a matter of weeks, and it seemed that I could look forward to the outcome of my Army medical in the following December without too much trepidation. I would make a point of bringing along the four X-rays and a letter from Dr Ranking when I appeared before the Medical Board in Maidstone. It was a bit of luck, too, that my Uncle Jack should have known someone on that Board, pointing out that I had just had pleurisy. And, indeed, three months later, I was graded C3, so that, for the time being – and in wartime, every day, every week, every month counts – I would be safe from the Services. Meanwhile, on that hot afternoon of mid-September, I could hold on to the reassurance of convalescence. I was not as convalescent as big Jim, I was indeed on the road to recovery, but it looked like being a fairly long road. And, of course, there was much to be said for the company of someone who was in a much worse medical condition than myself; in the third week of the war, there was a sort of comfort in being with someone whom it would pass by. So I was glad to have got to know Jim just at that time. He had only come down to Tunbridge Wells the week before; and his passive participation as an onlooker in the blackberrying was his first outing. It had been authorized, after some debate and telephone calls to Jim's father, by Nancy's father, also a doctor.

Jim's condition and company were not the only crumb of hope in that desperate month. Just about then my brother-in-law had obtained for himself a Reserved Occupation and had moved from the coast – Chatham was very much a place to be avoided in the conditions of September 1939 – with my sister and their baby to Hemingford Abbots, a quiet village on the Huntingdonshire Ouse. The black hat, the heavy mac, the dark suit and the spats were the outward symbols of my reasonable hopes for the next few months or so. By dressing almost as a parody of a civilian, I managed to feel myself even *more* civilian. Certainly I never applied so much energy and enthusiasm to blackberrying as on that sunny, cloudless afternoon. One could not have imagined a less warlike activity, it was something seasonal, like excursions to the primrose woods on the edge of the Bayham Estate, in March or April, blackberries had nothing to do with the War Effort – a menacing phrase then just making its unlovely appearance in officialese – and, as if to spite official priorities, the blackberries were particularly succulent and juicy that year.

I am not attempting to read too much into the two little photos, they are not problem pictures, they tell their own story quite clearly, even over a gulf of fifty years. I knew myself then, and I know myself now. I have not changed very much, I am merely forty-nine years older, and no longer in need of dressing myself up as middle-aged, I *am* middle-aged, and look it, indeed, I am even on the far side of that once so ardently desired state (I cannot think of any prospect more forbidding than being all at once projected back into my twenty-third year, or into *any* of my twenties, a decade that put me at almost constant physical risk and that only released me from uniform at the age of twenty-nine: no thanks, there would be no going back *that* way!). I was very frightened then, feeling threatened by the relentlessness of public events, so that I clung rather desperately to any scrap of reassurance that could be derived from private activities: in the last three months of 1939 and the first two months of 1940, I wrote up my B.Litt. thesis on François-Nicolas Vincent, a minor terrorist and a man of extreme violence who was executed, along with the other so-called *hébertistes*, in the Spring of 1794, a fate that he richly deserved; writing it up was a form of escape from the present, the first of many subsequent *fuites en arrière*, and in this it was altogether successful, I became so deeply immersed that I was only dimly aware of the Winter War. As an academic exercise, however, it was a complete failure; my thesis, which was badly written, and in which I made far too many claims for its unpleasant subject, was quite rightly referred, and, on my return to Paris in 1946, I abandoned Vincent for good.

I had every reason to be frightened in the autumn and winter of 1939, and I am sure I was not alone in my fears. I think this was one of the reasons why those in my age group at the time were often so desperate to seek out one another's company, there seemed to be some sort of consolation in numbers, we were, as it might have been said, 'in it together' (the very *last* thing I wanted to be in, in fact, 'togetherness' has never been my strong suit, and, at one point, I think in 1940, I was to be offered the quite blissful prospect of 'being out of it alone'); still, one could discuss possible routes of escape. And I have remained something of a catastrophist ever since. Perhaps now I live less in fear of war and revolution, though the prospect of potential class war in this country sometimes haunts me: I am firmly rooted in the English middle-classes – indeed, I have never felt more English nor more middle-class, and this is intended very much as a middle-class chronicle, perhaps another *fuite en arrière* – yet I am all too well aware that this may constitute a rickety stockade offering only flimsy security and that could so easily be breached by the forces of envy and social rancour; and it would take no great effort of imagination to envisage a situation in which one found oneself caught in the trap of a bitterly divided and dangerous island. It had all happened before, I had been denied the wonderful promise of a safe haven in Portugal, teaching at a prep school at Carcavelhos (I had even been given a contract), in 1940 or 1941 – I was refused an exit permit – and it could all happen again, though at least now I am well past the age of military service. There are *some* advantages in getting old: I can still recall my sense of relief at reaching the age of fifty-five. It is only in my still recurring nightmares that I find myself all at once remobilised and back in uniform, even with a pretty convincing W.O. Class Two's 'poached egg' on my sleeves (in my dreams, I ask myself if it would help to put matters right if I were to sew on my France Germany Star, and my other medals – what about the Legion? – on my tunic, surely this would help to indicate my age?), waking from sleep in a sweat, and in a mixture of fear and indignation at such personal injustice: surely, at seventy, I might be able to count on the State leaving me alone, and allowing me to dress as I wish?

Meanwhile, I still endeavour to erect what feeble barriers I can in order to contain the implacability of the public chronicle and of collective orthodoxies. There is, of course, the comfort of the family, very much a private enterprise, a fragile *fuite en avant*, a timid bid on an uncertain future, and perhaps the most effective refuge from collectivism and from the threats of the crowd. But, on that sunny afternoon in mid-September, blackberrying offered at least a residual guarantee that things would go on as before and that the seasons would repeat themselves. In fact, things did not go on quite as before: in September 1940, I found myself in Blackpool, teaching Polish airmen English, and there were no blackberries to be seen anywhere along the Golden Mile, or, as far as I could calculate, anywhere in the sandy Fylde. Still, one had to make do with any prop that came readily to hand; in 1939, it had been blackberries, in 1940, it would be quiet walks on my own in a still unspoiled countryside the other side of Fleetwood, or large teas in reassuringly middle-class hotels in Lytham St Anne's.

How desperately we cling to the familiar and the routinal, and never more so than in periods of public peril, crisis, and war! Blackberrying on that sunny afternoon in mid-September had represented a bid to escape, for a few hours at least, from the screaming chronicle of war, as well as the promise of renewal, a timid effort to pre-empt an uncertain future. Middle-class hotels in Lytham St Anne's carried their own message of reassurance, because they *were* so solidly middle-class, it was a bit like visiting old friends. September 1939 set me determinedly, evening after evening, generally around eight o'clock, along past the two little stone crocodiles with their two little stone mounts holding their rusted cross-bows: sentinels to the still recent memory of a secure childhood and so to the promise of a safety now imperilled, along the dark, unmade road, past the fields that skirted Camden Park from behind, past the house of Mrs Park, the General's widow, who, in the daytime, could always be seen wearing one of her late-husband's old brown trilbies, to Rookley, the big house set in its own extensive grounds, on the sharp corner opposite the Hawkenbury turn. What brought me there, night after night, in 1939 and 1940, was the need to talk, to seek out company in an effort, I suppose, if not to eliminate, at least to cover over, the awful reality of war. I knew exactly whom I would find in the big, drafty drawing-room, a rough extension of the house that looked and felt as if it had been built on as a hurried after-thought, even where each would be sitting, and there was a sort of calm reassurance in Jim's massive presence, for, by now, things had moved on at some speed from the afternoon when he had sat in the back of the car while we had busied ourselves filling our little baskets, and he had become part of the house, and would indeed before long be married to it: as I saw it, a private act of defiance that flew in the face of stated public priorities and Fougasse posters, and an assertion of faith in family survival. Jim, once married to Nancy some time early in 1940, seemed to *anchor* the big house in a comfortable sort of predictability. Anchor was the right word, for, before his illness, he had enjoyed playing with boats in his parents' country place on or near Southampton Water, and there was a ship's bell over the front-door which I was in the habit of ringing, after I had come in by the back gate on the side-road, past the sheds, and had crossed the dark

garden, over the croquet lawn, not to be let in – I would let myself in –
but to signal my presence to those inside behind the thick green
black-out curtains.

Rookley, during the early war years – later the house was
requisitioned by some Government agency – became a substitute
Percy House, my welcoming evening terminus when in Tunbridge
Wells, another home from home. And it would continue in that role
long after the war was over and I no longer went there in search of
reassurance through endless talk, but out of friendship and affection,
and, on visits at tea-time, to see the three children in the nursery far
upstairs. I had first set foot in the place, for a children's Christmas
treasure hunt, at the age of fourteen, so that it had carried me right
through the dangerous years till I had reached firmer, safer ground, at
the age of thirty. The ship's bell had spelt out safety, the huge
porcelain figures of the Chinese mandarins, with their long, straggl-
ing, curly black beards made of some sort of coarse cotton, asserted
by their presence that everything was as it should be and that nothing
much had changed (indeed, the temporary residents, evacuees, I
think, had gone back to where they had come from, and the original
inhabitants had returned). I felt grateful to the mandarins, they
seemed to affirm civilian priorities.

I had no fear of the pitch black dark, returning back along the
unmade road, sometimes as late as midnight, the only sound the
gentle breathing of the cows, as they slept in the fields behind
Camden Park, serene guardians of the big grey doctors' houses. I
knew every inch of the road, every contour, the position of every
lamp-post, and I could feel the approach of the sudden rise of the
uneven pavement. I had managed to do without a torch during the
black-out years. But how welcoming the three lamp-posts, once more
throwing out their feeble yellow light, after them! On all my
innumerable trips to and from Rookley, I had never met a soul, no
one came that way at night, the road belonged to me, and to me
alone, like the cows, it breathed out peace. It was getting there and
getting back that was as enjoyable and as soothing as the conversation once I had reached my destination. The wonderful stillness was
the gentle prelude to untroubled sleep. I haven't been that way for
many years now, Rookley has gone, it was pulled down many years

ago, half-a-dozen houses have been built in what had been the big garden, perhaps the road itself has lost its still, almost secret tranquility. Best not to try and find out, it is generally a mistake to go back.

There were other regular evening itineraries within Tunbridge Wells, though none so personal, so totally enfolding as the dark road to Rookley. During much of the 1950s and the early 1960s in the vacations I would take the steep road up past the Five Ways, to the George, an elegant pub-hotel just below the level of the London Road, to meet a friend who taught German at Skinner's School. It was a truncated, evening version of my many climbs, over a much longer period, up to Percy House. In my dependence on such evening itineraries on 'getting out' and seeking company, after supper, I seem to have been a bit like my Uncle Jack, the doctor, always eager to get into his car, and to respond to some urgent late-night call. Unlike him, however, I was not married.

In my years in Paris, too, especially after the war, there was a fairly regular weekly pattern of itineraries within the city, or beyond it, suggestive of a certain restlessness and an innate *loneliness*. Yet I also valued that loneliness, because it, too, brought the contrary promises of the familiar and the unknown. I became habituated to a sort of cuckoo existence, sampling especially on Sundays, other peoples' houses: 103, Avenue de Paris, Dourdan, a house always full of children, with a wild garden and many swings and hiding-places, a see-saw, rope ladders to get high up into the big trees, there were a couple of ash and an oak. The house was next to a formal, regimented municipal park in the seventeenth-century French manner, as if in reproach to the happy untidiness of the tulgy playground on the other side of the stone wall. The house belonged to a local historian, M Emile Auvray, who had written a history of the Revolution in Dourdan and who had taught for many years at the local *Collège*. I had got to know him through the French Revolution which, in the past, had often served me well in this respect. M Auvray was one of a number of *érudits locaux* I had met as a result of common historical interests. What distinguished M Auvray from his fellow local historians was the fact that he didn't have a nose, he had lost it at some earlier stage, I never discovered how, he just had nostrils. One soon got used to the absence of the nose. He would meet me at the station, his white hair waving in the breeze – Dourdan is on the edge of the Beauce – and smiling; we would walk to the house below the curling line of the ramparts. There would just be time for *apéritifs*, of which there would be a wide choice, in the garden, with M Auvray's daughter and her husband, Théo, when he was on leave from the Côte-d'Ivoire. Mme Auvray, busy in the kitchen, would not emerge till lunch was ready. This was always an enormous affair, five courses, many plates, many glasses, laid out in splendour in the dining-room. After lunch, an energetic walk in the broom-covered chalky hills, as an addition to the *digestifs*, then back to the house for the six o'clock *apéritifs*, followed by a cold supper in the little room on the other side of the corridor from the dark, well-shuttered dining-room, which was not yet in use, the table still bearing evidence to the luncheon battlefield. I think this must have been the only time in the week in which the room opposite was used for meals. Piles of schoolbooks, exercise books, colouring books, children's comics, and back numbers of fashion magazines would be temporarily expelled from the table to make room for the plates and bottles. Apart from being cold, supper could compete, in respect of volume and variety, on pretty even terms with lunch. After supper, and generally with very little time to spare, M Auvray, walking as fast as his short legs would carry him, would accompany me back to the station, taking the road below the curling ramparts, for the last train back to Paris. I generally fell asleep on the train, but always managed to wake up at my stop, Saint-Michel. Nothing could beat a Dourdan Sunday: I liked the journey there, the little stations with increasingly pretty rural-sounding names once one was beyond the rather sinister Juvisy, I liked my little noseless friend (who made up in assertiveness – he didn't like being contradicted, especially on points of fact, and his son-in-law took a mischievous delight in contradicting him – for his small stature), I liked his wife – they were both from the Pas-de-Calais and had retained the harsh accent of their common origins – their rather solemn daughter, a teacher (almost inevitably), their easy-going son-in-law, and their wonderfully energetic children. I think of Dourdan every time I cross the quay by the entrance to the underground station Saint-Michel; but I have never returned there. It seemed best not to risk it. The house might have been pulled down, the roof leaked badly, the garden could have been tidied up, the trees might have come down in a gale, or strangers might have moved in. It was best not to know what had happened.

For other Sundays, for a period of eight to ten years, there was a grey stucco villa called something like *Villa Minouchette* – I know it was a diminutive and I am sure it was engagingly ridiculous, it also had a bizarre number, 19 ter – in a quiet avenue of Le Vésinet. The avenue led to a little municipal park that was called *Les Ibis*. In the park there were fifteen or sixteen stone cranes perched on their concrete legs amidst foliage on a series of artificial islands linked by Japanese-style miniature bridges in cement made to look like rough wood. The islands were dotted, in studied irregularity, in an oblong lake with a concrete bottom. I suppose the cranes had been erected to lend substance to the name given to the park. The park was approached by a small *rond point* constructed around a stone statue, on a plinth, of an enormous stag proudly raising his cement antlers and staring haughtily down the avenue, with his back to the park. On the edge of the park there was a huge white and green house in the moorish manner with little metal minarets, the home of a chocolate millionaire. The whole effect, I thought, made up most convincing Queneau country. But my friends did not read Queneau, they did not read novels, they thought they were frivolous, and certainly not conducive to militancy.

Minouchette was the improbable home of Lucien and Natasha Weitz (née Mjakotina), a Franco-Russian couple who personified the equally improbable match of an improvident and gesticulatory cosmopolitanism and a prudent, not to say mean, French petit-bourgeois provincialism. The neighbourhood, the villa itself (straight out of the early twenties), and its name all seemed an odd choice for a couple who continued to talk revolution (both at once), from morning to night, right through meals, through walks in *Les Ibis* (where Natasha would hold forth in her guttural and strangely accented French, waving her arms to give dramatic effect to a tirade, as if she had been trying to win over the stone cranes). But, in fact, the choice had not been theirs. The villa had been built by Lucien's father, a pale, rather colourless blonde man, always dressed in a grey suit and brown bedroom slippers, with a grey cap on his head, a retired grocer from somewhere in Lower Normandy who was still living with them when I first got to know them and who would munch quietly, but doggedly – he had rather loose-fitting dentures – through the mealtime double perorations, without ever raising his head from his plate. Another resident at that time was Natasha's aunt, Vera, the widow of a Tsarist naval officer, a staunch supporter of the old monarchy (her father, she would proudly declare, in halting French, had been *baisé par le Tsar*, a turn of phrase that always drew a laugh from the children) and a regular attender at the cathedral in the rue Daru. The villa was not very large, but somehow they had managed to cram everybody in. Lucien and Natasha had five children, four boys and a girl. The boys slept in unmade beds in one room, they never used sheets; the girl, Anna-Claire, had a room of her own. Lucien's father occupied the best room of the house – it was, after all, *his* house – it had a balcony looking out on a small orchard and the unkempt garden; but he never sat out on the balcony, and he had quite lost interest in the garden. The elderly aunt had a small, dark room on the ground-floor; in it there was a black-faced ikon with a red lamp burning in front of it. Lucien and Natasha slept in a room over Lucien's study and facing onto the avenue.

Lucien and Natasha represented, in their joint effort – it was difficult to decide who was the sillier of the two, though I think I would have put my money on the Russian – what must have been a pretty comprehensive encyclopaedia of political failure. There was something almost admirable in their consistent ability to back losers. Natasha may have inherited it, for her father, before and after the revolution, had been a leading figure among the S.Rs. Perhaps she had won over Lucien from the start. When they had first met, in Paris, in the early twenties, they had militated with *le capitaine* Treint; from Treint, they had switched to Boris Souvarine. They had naturally opposed Thorez from the start; no name was more hated, *Villa Minouchette*, than *le Fils du Peuple*, the Great Betrayer. They had drifted for a time on the vague borders of Trotskyism. Then they had rallied to Marceau Pivert, just at a time when he had begun losing out to the majority line represented, within the SFIO, by Léon Blum. By the time I had come to know them, they were probably the last two surviving *pivertistes*. In the late thirties Lucien had been organiser and secretary of the *Fédération de la Jeunesse Socialiste de la Seine*, a group that had been rejected, as being out of step, by the national organisation. Natasha and Lucien seemed to give flesh – not much flesh in the case of the former, she was very thin and angular – and blood to the word *minoritaires*. I suppose it was a form of pride, of having been right all along. I believe that, left to his own devices, Lucien might occasionally have strayed in the direction of the big battalions; but with Natasha constantly at his side, as a sort of high priestess of political purity, there would be little danger of his ever coming out on the winning side. By the time I had got to know them in the early 1950s, they had revised their view of Léon Blum, even expressing a lingering affection for *le Grand Léon*, whose public career had by then ended in political failure. The new demon figure was Guy Mollet, the man who had got the better of Blum. A regular visitor to the villa was Georges Boris, who had been Blum's *chef de cabinet* at the time of the formation of the Popular Front Government; Boris had sunk almost without a trace in the post-war political scene. For a couple who lived for politics – they certainly did not live off them – there was something almost touching in their unerring ability to get everything wrong. I think they regarded political success as the mark of Cain. After the Liberation of North Africa, Lucien had become the first – and last – editor of *Alger Soir*, a Left-wing daily at once rejected by the PCA, by the more moderate Algerian nationalists, the followers of Messali Haj, and the majority of the *pieds noirs*. The paper had soon folded for lack of readers. He attributed the collapse of this no doubt worthy enterprise to the obscene alliance of the Algerian Communist Party and of the various settlers' pressure groups.

Once back in France, he had found employment as advertising editor of *La Revue des Mines*, the official trade journal of *Les Charbonnages de France* and of the mining engineers. When it was pointed out to him that this was an odd position for a convinced revolutionary, with twenty years of (mostly futile) militancy behind him, he would argue that capitalism could best be destroyed from within.

Sometime in the 1930s, he had attended a Fabian conference held in Balliol. This might have been a one-off event. But there was something badly out of focus about a Frenchman who then had made a habit of attending this sort of thing annually. At the first of these gatherings, he had been introduced to G. D. H. Cole, who had made a great fuss of him – I imagine Lucien was his only French disciple – and whom he visited on all his subsequent pilgrimages across the Channel. He took a touching pride in his friendship with the Sage of the Banbury Road, and he kept all the group photographs of these summer gatherings on the lawn of the Garden Quad. In all of these, one could spot him, fingering his pipe, seated in the front row; in two of them, he was even placed on the left of the great man himself. I think he regarded the photos as a series of sporting trophies of his political purity.

Lucien was a self-educated, self-satisfied *primaire*, lacking in imagination, prone to boasting in an effort to impress the first comer. He did not really exist in his own right, his main importance was to have been the husband of Natasha (perhaps he was vaguely aware of this himself, for, in the course of the summer following her death, while on holiday in the Cevennes, he was given to holding forth to total strangers, most of them Protestants from Nîmes, who would listen in polite bewilderment, about what a remarkable wife he had had. These embarrassing effusions would generally take place after lunch, on the terrace of the local hôtel-restaurant, and would be followed by the widower's copious and noisy tears). The effort may have been too much for him, for six months or so after her death, once back in Le Vésinet, he fell quite comfortably into an incurably petit-bourgeois way of life, setting up with a nondescript woman of Belgian origin, who looked after his creature comforts – like his father, he now took to wearing carpet-slippers throughout the day – and who had long set her eye on the villa for herself and her illegitimate son: she got it in the end, the reward of patience and of sitting it out. The flow of visitors to the house dried up almost at once. Lucien in the absence of Natasha was not a person one would go out of one's way to know. This was something that, in Natasha's lifetime, had been quite clearly perceived by the four sons and the daughter of the couple.

It was not difficult to see why the boys should have taken their cue from their mother; Lucien was a dull fellow, always convinced of his own wisdom. He was quick to lose his temper when neither his wife nor his sons showed any willingness to listen to him. His own success in life had been to marry Natasha (described to me, not very tactfully, as I hastened to suggest to them, at the time of Natasha's funeral – we were on our way to the *Columbarium* of the Père Lachaise – as *cette étrangère*, by Lucien's Norman relatives). It had been a very strange choice on her part, as she had previously moved in Surrealist circles, and had been associated closely – even intimately – with a whole series of prominent figures of the French and the cosmopolitan Left. Souvarine had been more than an ideological attraction, and, at some later stage, she had lived with the historian, Jean Dautry, at a time when he had been excluded, for some heresy or other, from the French Communist Party (later, having toed the line, he was allowed back in). Then I think there had been an interlude with Trotsky's son. Perhaps Lucien had eventually won the day simply because he had been so ordinary; his very ordinariness would have prevented him from ever competing on a footing of equality with his wonderfully flamboyant wife.

It was not very hard to take to Natasha, she was completely uncalculating, totally generous, and, often in spite of herself, great fun. There could be no doubt about her entertainment value, though to have been exposed to her regularly, day after day, night after night, might have been rather exhausting. I was only a Sunday visitor, and by no means on every Sunday, so I could measure out with some care my own degree of exposure to her performances. I am sure that she reserved the best of these for her enlarged, and, no doubt, more appreciative, Sunday audiences, and it is possible that, during the week, she actually took a bit of time off from dramatics, doing less walking up and down, and even sitting at table and eating, during meals, or what passed for meals. I had the freedom – as, indeed, I did with my friends in Dourdan – of being able to come and go as I pleased (there is every advantage in being a *visitor* to a house – a role I seem consistently to have occupied in much of the present account – than in being *visited* in one's own, a passive position much more exposed and over which one has less control, and one that, as a general rule of life, I have always tried my best to avoid. There is a wonderful feeling of security in the knowledge not only that there is a convenient point of exit readily available: 'don't bother to get up, I know the way, I'll let myself out', but that one can choose one's own time to use it. It was also a role well suited to my own favourite stance, and one that I still endeavour to preserve, as an observer prudently placed somewhere on the sidelines, rather than as a participant in the thick of things and becoming too closely involved; one can observe – and listen – best from a little distance.). Confined within fortnightly and three-weekly intervals, there could be no doubt about Natasha's entertainment value, and she often came out with statements so utterly extravagant that they set me into fits. She didn't mind being laughed at, taking it, I think, as a compliment.

I felt that there was even something to be said for Lucien; he was at least a convinced anglophile, even if that took the form of being an admirer of G. D. H. Cole and of attending annual Fabian Conferences, sitting on the ground, cross-legged, or with knees up in the Garden Quad of Balliol: one should not be too demanding, French anglophiles, of whatever political persuasion, are rare enough. And I became very fond of some of the children, especially Anna-Claire, who had plenty of common sense, and of Roland, the third brother, who had absolutely none, and who was the only member of the family to have no intellectual pretentions whatsoever and to show no interest in politics of any kind.

In Paris my itineraries, both in the time I was living there throughout the year, and as recalled in a tenacious memory, were also closely linked to the *métro*, a network that imposes its own entirely familiar succession of names and that one ends up greeting like old friends. Just as, by pushing a coloured button on one of the more elaborate *plans du métro*, one lights up a whole line – Vincennes-Pont de Neuilly, Porte d'Orleans-Porte de Clignancourt, I wish I could remember the twin of Balard – in a series of shining yellow dots, so for me, over the years, certain stops would light up with the expectancy of familiarity, the strong likelihood of certain encounters, the sure guarantee of friendship, affection and greeting, the promise of someone to listen to and who would make me, and others, laugh: *TERNES*: the stately, exquisitely polite Monsieur Alexandre – held locally in such high esteem as to be denied the banality of a surname – *vieille France* in person, with his gold-topped stick, his red *rosette* showing up on his rather shiny blue suit,

23

standing at the counter, Café-Tabac des Acacias, in the street of the same name; one could not count absolutely on his presence at his generally recognized post, there were periods of months when he would not be seen, absent *en villégiature*, as he expressed it delicately, and no one would have had the bad taste to press him on the locality of his rural retreat; then he would be back again, his normal very high colour somewhat paled, taking up the thread of the conversation in his ancien régime French where he had left off six months or a year previously. His Months in the Country never amounted to *more* than a year. And outside, and visible from the café, *la grosse Fernande* – the name seemed somehow to designate her outsize appearance and boisterous character, so much so that I cannot imagine a Fernande who was thin, small, discreet, or silent – a big girl of outstanding vulgarity, speaking the Parisian of La Chapelle, always in good humour, and endowed with a capacity to fart very loudly to order, on her assigned beat, whatever the weather. But sometimes she would come into the café, out of the rain, closing her dripping violet and yellow umbrella, ordering for herself a *vittel-fraise*, and followed by her self-made deep blasts of thunder, as she exchanged cheerful remarks in doubtful taste with the regular customers of this well-placed outpost (the café was on a corner, facing onto the rue des Acacias and the Avenue des Ternes, a double observatory of the Parisian night). Fernande, too, had her periods of absence, *en villégiature* I think in a different place from that favoured by Monsieur Alexandre; but both seemed to have been creatures of habit. Fernande always came back apparently refreshed, her high spirits and her exuberant vulgarity undimmed.

OBLIGADO (as it then was, it is now *ARGENTINE*): my friend, Maurice Chauvirey, wearing his specially made cats'-fur waistcoat (the winters of 1946 and of 1947 carrying the memory of savage cold, the wind from the East sweeping down the Avenue de la Grande Armée, providing the chilling advance columns of the expected Cossacks, wrapped up in furs, mounted on their little horses, and heading fast and purposefully westwards, in the direction of Neuilly; the wind seemed to announce the imminence of their arrival, but they never came, neither that winter, nor the next one, nor the one after that) and his brown hat, set at a jaunty, impudent angle, that he kept on even indoors, to cover his large, very round, very bald, very red head. Maurice, a comparative newcomer to the Quartier des Ternes – prosperity in the Black Market had brought him here in the last year of the Occupation – had introduced me to *la grosse Fernande*, pinching her ample and resonant bottom, to a number of her colleagues, and to the courteous Monsieur Alexandre.

FRANKLIN-D-ROOSEVELT: the assurance of a double welcome, the illusion, too, of a family responsibility – it may indeed have contained quite a few elements of reality, so regular were my evening visits, and so deeply was I taken into the confidence of both: the twelve-year-old Irène, a pretty, very intelligent child, with very dark hair, setting off her pale skin, and very black eyes, the whites of which were unusually large and expressive and which she was able to roll, apparently at will, to give herself a comic appearance: half-Greek, half-Welsh, and her mother, Mme Thomas, wholly Greek. Irène and her mother lived in a large single-room studio flat, with a tiny kitchen and bathroom off it, and which faced away from the Avenue, onto the backs of other blocks of 1930 constructions. Mother and daughter spoke French together, as well as to me. Irène's father had met her mother, then still a schoolgirl, in 1919 in Constantinople, where he had been teaching English. Before that he had been in the army, but Mme Thomas had been uncertain in what rank, she had thought he had been an officer, but I had my doubts. Anyhow, he had done quite well for himself, marrying into an affluent family of local Greeks, the Papandopouloses; on the subject of his own family background in South Wales he had apparently been rather reticent. At some stage, they had come to France with their small daughter. The father had been shot by the Germans, near Grenoble, in 1943, accused of having spied for the British – later, the War Office was to claim no knowledge either of him or of the organisation on behalf of which he had claimed to have worked, and had refused to grant his widow a pension. I was told about all this very early on, when I had first got to know Mme Thomas and Irène, in 1945 or 1946, and had done what I could, which had not been very much. She told me that she had never known what her husband had been up to from 1940 to 1943. He seemed to have been a pretty bad husband, and he had never been very truthful: that she had found at a very early stage of their marriage.

Mme Thomas looked permanently worried; worry rather suited her, giving her a wistful look and a timid, uncertain, apologetic smile. There was a thin tracery of worry around her eyes. She did not look as if she could cope. Indeed, she appeared so lost, bewildered and defenceless that the people at the embassy – she and Irène were British subjects – took pity on her, finding her a secretarial post with NATO, then still in Paris, housed in huts below the Palais de Chaillot. In any case, she was not as defenceless and as lonely as the apparent existence of the bereaved couple, widowed mother and orphaned daughter, living in a single room – albeit a very big one, well-heated and well-appointed, in a building facing onto the old Avenue Victor-Emmanuel III – might have at first suggested to the casual visitor. The Papandopoulos clan was present in strength. Mlle Cara, Mme Thomas's aunt, who taught the piano to young ladies from the XVIme, and who had been a pupil of the celebrated Gieseking – Mlle Cara told me that he had been celebrated – lived in the studio-flat on the other side of the first-floor landing. I had known Mlle Cara before the war, when she had shared a small flat near Saint-Augustin with a German lady, Mlle Goetz, who had been my German teacher. During the Occupation, Mlle Cara had been denounced, but, having been forewarned by a friendly *commissaire de police*, she had been able to go into hiding. She thought she might have been denounced by Mlle Goetz, who, in 1941, had managed to obtain sole possession of the studio-flat on the Avenue Victor-Emmanuel III. On returning to Paris for the first time in October 1944, I had called on Mlle Cara, who had told me all about my former German teacher and what she, Edith Goetz, had been up to, and who had introduced me to her niece and her great-niece, living just opposite. So I could indeed claim to have been an old friend of the family. Mme Thomas's mother, her two sisters, and her brother, Thalis, were also living in Paris, in a large appartment, rue Lafayette.

On Thursday afternoons, I was in the habit of taking Irène to the Bois or to the Luxembourg, then to a *pâtisserie*. I much enjoyed these excursions, they gave me the illusion, without the wear and tear of the real thing, of parenthood; it was quite fun to be a Thursday afternoon father, and Irène was very good company, prattling on about her friends at school, and keeping me up with the latest school slang. Apart from Thursdays, I often went there on Saturday and on Sunday. In the evening I would stay on at the studio until it was time for Irène and her mother to be going to bed. I would leave just as they were letting down a collapsible bed that fitted into a sort of cupboard in the wall. This was always the signal for me to depart. I would head back to *FRANKLIN-D-ROOSEVELT* with a comfortable family feeling. But I lost touch with mother and daughter and the big studio when Irène was fifteen. The two of them moved after that to a small flat in the wastes around the Ecole Militaire. Several years later, Irène married the manager of the Hôtel du Pont-Royal (the bar of which was a favourite meeting-place for Gallimard authors). Irène had done very well for herself, and her mother was very pleased. There was a big wedding at the Lutheran church of Les Billettes. I was glad at least that my small companion on the walks in the Bois or the Luxembourg had married a Protestant. So, I gathered, were the Papandopouloses.

To return to the *métro* and its itineraries there was also, for instance, the long pull, with one change, via *MICHEL-ANGE-MOLITOR*, from *ODEON* to *MARCEL-SEMBAT*, that, for several years, gave a clear identity to Sunday morning, culminating in the little, two-storeyed, so very provincial, grey house, at the top end of the Avenue Jean-Jaurès, the home of *Le Vieux Maître*, the historian, Georges Lefebvre, whom Soboul and I were in the habit of visiting the first Sunday of each month, arriving at the hour of eleven, and leaving at half-past twelve, after having been offered two or three glasses of bitter Noilly-Prat. If our *directeur de thèses* expressed guarded – it would never have been anything more than that, he was not given to excess – approval of what we claimed to have achieved since our previous visit, I would reward myself by having lunch on my own in a small *restaurant d'habitués* a few doors up from the house on the same side of the Avenue Jean-Jaurès. It made a nice change from Dourdan or Le Vésinet. I liked regular itineraries, but the art was to vary them a bit.

One could never associate the *métro* with threat, not then anyhow, it represented the map, just below the surface, sometimes high above the roof-tops, of journeys regularly undertaken, in the knowledge of a welcome at the far end, then of the return, among a few sleepy passengers, to the comfort and safety of bed. As one emerged below the aggressive and posturing statue of Danton – *de l'audace, encore de l'audace*, and all that – it was indeed the sense of returning home, to base. Danton was like a familiar lighthouse, a symbol of peace, the promise of sleep. How often would I emerge there, just before the *métro* closed for the night, in the late 1940s and the early 1950s, having travelled back from Mme Thomas's, changing at *CON-CORDE*! There would be other regular destinations, on the outward journey: *PORTE DE CHARENTON, PORTE DE VERSAILLES, BALARD, PORTE D'ORLEANS*, indeed most places save *PIGALLE* or *BLANCHE*. The poesy of the *métro* draws heavily both on its familiarity and its banality, its *ordinariness*: it is hard to take *FILLES DU CALVAIRE* seriously, *SEVRES-BABYLONE* poses no threat, *SOLFERINO, CHAMBRE DES DEPUTES*, as seen from below ground, are entirely unprestigious. *LOURMEL*, despite its vague promise of aristocratic distinction, is seen only in passing; it is somewhere I have never got out at. *MALESHERBES*, on the other hand, offers the prospect of comfortable wealth, slow-moving, roomy lifts and carpeted stairs, of medical reassurance (especially during my hepatic period of the early 1950s when I used to consult a liver specialist there: he was much more interested in Marat, a doctor of sorts, than in my liver) and of very good china tea with a retired cavalry General, who was also a historian and an antique-dealer, and who lived in a flat crammed with medieval ecclesiastical statues, reredoses and pictures, rue Jacques-Bingen, opposite the Soviet Trade Mission.

STRASBOURG-SAINT-DENIS represents the promise of the end of the month Friday girls, indeed, of one particular girl, nicknamed *Gaby la Landaise* (like Monsieur Alexandre, she seems to have gone through life, in her case, brief, without the benefit of a surname), the object of my evening visits on the last Friday of the month, when I had been paid: *Hôtel du Centre*, on the corner of the Porte Saint-Denis and the rue d'Aboukir. I liked Gaby, a good-looking girl with high cheek-bones and a delicate bone structure, well-spoken, intelligent, and amusing; and I was always prepared to wait till she was free, *l'affaire d'un instant*, the *patronne* would assure me. I did not have to tell whom I was waiting for. I called on

Gaby I suppose something like twelve or thirteen Fridays, anyhow, just over a year. Then, one Friday, I asked the *patronne* if I would have long to wait; she said that I would indeed. Gaby was no longer there, nor anywhere. The week before, she had shot herself, placing a revolver in her mouth, in one of the sparse bedrooms on the fifth floor, No 78. There had been trouble with her man. She seemed genuinely upset, commenting that Gaby had been a well-educated girl, more than her *certificat d'études primaires*, perhaps even a *bachelière*, that she came from a very good home, and that her parents had a large shop – a grocery – in Dax. Gaby was only twenty-seven when she shot herself. Over the last forty years, she has often been in my thoughts, and I can still recall the unusual, rather striking lines of her face. She was amusing and observant and always seemed good-humoured. I think I most liked talking to her, we would start up much at the point at which we had left off, a month before. It seemed such a brutally short life. That was the end of *STRASBOURG-SAINT-DENIS* as far as my monthly Friday visits were concerned. After that, I moved further west, to *RUE-MONMARTRE* or *RICHELIEU-DROUOT* (*VAVIN* or the appropriately named *GAITE* might offer similar services, there was something to be said for varying the Banks).

So, on the whole, the *carte du métro* represents, or used to represent, an ever-reliable map of reassurance, familiarity, and often, as in the case of *GAITE*, appropriateness: *GLACIERE* really is what it says it is, *NATIONALE*, as one would expect of that adjective, is scruffy, run-down and dreary, even if the old, sculpted, filigreed carriages of the *Nord-Sud* (so much in that name, too, a monument to Paris–1900) have been replaced, and *ORLEANS-CLIGNANCOURT* has become *inodore*, and the little *Dubo, Dubon, Dubonnet* man, in his bowler, raising his glass and emptying it *d'un seul trait*, has long since disappeared from the tunnels. How suitable that the evocation of the *métro* should have played such a large part in the literature of exile, during the Occupation years, in the pages of the London monthly, *La France Libre*! How appropriate, too, that, in his recollections of a very deprived childhood in the XIIIme *arrondissement*, the populist writer and *argotier*, Alphonse Boudard, should have associated the *métro* with his generally

unsuccessful pursuit, as a pimply sixteen-year-old, of girls encountered in the favourable conditions, below ground, of the evening
rush-hour: ('She got out at *PLACE D'ITALIE*, unfortunately she
took the corridor *DIRECTION ETOILE*, and I was heading
NATION'), the surest enthronement in individual memory.

Regular itineraries then represent the fragile barriers erected by the
timid and the fearful, people like myself, in a modest endeavour to
keep at bay the relentlessness of public events, and the orthodoxies of
totalitarianism. I have become as much attached to the *carte du métro*,
within its old boundaries, because it is a map that has managed
somehow to freeze, to immobilize, the continuity from the last years of
the Third Republic, through the triumphant Occupation years (1943
being the apotheosis), to the present time, as I was, in the 1950s and the
1960s, to the two *ficelles* that connected La Croix-Rousse to Les
Terreaux and that lent a deceptively reassuring topography to *l'affaire
de Caluire*, the arrest of Jean Moulin and of *le général* Delestraint, in
1943. Had not one of the participants at that fatal meeting taken the
more eastern *ficelle* up the hill? I think it could have been the same
almost anywhere, and not just in Paris or Lyon. When, for instance, I
recall Columbia, South Carolina, what identifies the place as far as I
am concerned, is a steep, sunny step down from the terrace of an ice-
cream parlour and a small bar and eatery, down to the level of the street
that formed part of the little shopping complex of Five Points. I grew
attached to the steep step because I knew that it was there, and that I
had to negotiate it with caution. It became as much part of a personal
local topography as the six steps leading down from the level of the
quay of the Saône, near the Pont La Feuillée, Quartier Saint-Paul, in
Lyon, to the cafés, the restaurants, the little shops and the houses on
the street that are several feet lower than the road itself. I recall in
particular a restaurant, narrow and deep, from the vantage point of
which one could only see the passing traffic: lorries, cars, buses,
motorcycles halfway up, their tops concealed, giving the little restaurant an agreeably subterranean feeling, as if it had been constantly in
the process of sinking further and further into the ground.

There are many other places: Rouen, Roubaix, Le Havre, Dieppe,
Marseille, Brussels, that I have likewise succeeded in disciplining to
topographies of reassurance and predictability. Oxford, however,

has eluded me. Not so Cambridge, a place I associate with bitterly cold and misty February mornings and many cyclists, darting in both directions down the narrow lanes between close-packed colleges and the Regent House, their numbers and their urgency increasing on the stroke of the hour – nine or ten o'clock (from Trinity, from King's, from the University church, from Caius) – as I make my weekly way towards the ring road, to my lecture-room in West Road, meeting, at the level of the English Faculty, crocodiles of little boys in caps and blazers, as they head in the opposite direction. The numbers and the urgency of the cyclists gave me the agreeable impression that I was indeed walking and breathing to Cambridge Full Term time: but a Cambridge permanently stuck in February and March mornings, the cyclists with their breath visible in the sharp air, the big, ghostly trees festooned with white. The place had admitted me because I stuck to a regular schedule and because I was heading in much the same direction as perhaps half of the eager armies of cyclists, their bells tinkling, their baskets full of books and notes. So I was part of the general rhythm of work. I found this both exciting and satisfying because, previously, I had only observed Cambridge as a visitor, and now I was a participant. Perhaps, too, almost by accident, I had stumbled on one of the secrets of that university town, its uniqueness a rhythm of movement much more generalized than that imposed by a slower-moving, more lethargic, more college-bound Oxford, the awareness that, just before the stroke of each hour, young people crossed the town to attend first one lecture, then another, then a third. I liked thus to feel part of the general movement, caught up in it, carried along by it, in exactly the same way as I had early become habituated to the bizarre Aberystwyth custom of 'kicking bar'. I suppose I would have achieved full native status if I too had been on a bicycle, and not on foot. As a mere pedestrian, I did not entirely belong; and I could not help admiring the skill of the cyclists in avoiding one another while not observing any discipline of right or left in the narrow alleyways as they pedalled so determinedly in the one direction or the other, weaving effortlessly between bollards and through narrow gates and passage-ways, and thus establishing their own full *droits de cité* in a University town which is also still a market town and the centre for a well-defined and very beautiful agricultural region.

I suppose there is some sort of hidden chemistry about towns, capitals, ports, provincial centres. In Paris I used to feel it the most (it has largely gone now, for there is no chemistry at all about *voies piétonnes*, the mark of death for a once-living, unassuming street, about a dehumanized rue Quincampoix, a *cloître* Saint-Merri given over to the antics of jugglers and guitar-players, a rue Mouffetard invaded by strolling players, pseudo-mummers and strident orchestras, as they compete successfully with the organ of Saint-Médard). But I have felt it almost as much in Roubaix, coming towards the centre from Wasquehal and the canal; in Brussels, when approaching the *Ville Haute*; in Lyon, always climbing up steps, or coming down them, a city of innumerable *montées* and offering many unexpected perspectives over red-tiled roofs cascading unevenly far below; in Marseille, coming down from Endoum, or amidst the noise and bustle of the rue des Phocéens, an intimate thoroughfare in which the present-day *Phocéens* appear still to thrive; in Rouen, quartier Martainville; or Eau-de-Robec, a city which reveals most on its fringes, and least in its centre: the impersonal rue Thiers, the equally impersonal rue Jeanne-d'Arc; in Dieppe, in the narrow, secret streets of tall, gaunt houses in small grey bricks, behind the quays, and hidden by them: L'Enfer; even in the apparently unpromising Le Havre, once one has climbed up to the heights of Sanvic or Graville. And there are traces of it still, though less vivacious, less varied, less pungent, less noisy, more anonymous, more restrained, than at the time of his schooldays as an *interne* in the *lycée Clemenceau*, in the 1920s, of Julien Gracq's Nantes, a city then traversed, cut in two (as it still was when I went there in the 1950s) by the main line from Paris to Quimper, as described, in his recent masterpiece, *La forme d'une ville*.

TWO

The House in the Hythe

MY GRANDPARENTS, Charles and Catharine Cobb, managed to prolong the nineteenth century into the first twenty-six years of the present one. Or it could be put the other way round: that they succeeded in excluding the twentieth century pretty well up to the year 1926. Certainly their daily timetable and general manner of life could be taken as a warning to historians not to attach too much importance to the beginning or the end of a century as a particularly significant dividing line in neatly cut-up periods. My grandparents were Victorians, and remained so under Edward VII and George V; indeed my grandfather was born in 1837, as if to emphasize the fact (my grandmother, one year older, dated back to William IV). So they were among the minority of people scarcely to have been affected by the First World War, an event of which they must, however, have been aware, as their eldest son, Primus, who had always lived at home, and had never done any work after spending one year as a ship's engineer as a young man, went to work at Paxman's munition factory (it was just beyond the garden), and my grandfather had had himself driven over in his gig to White Colne, to see the still smoking remains of a Zeppelin that had been shot down. Moreover he would have had to interrupt his biannual business trips to Brussels (via Parkeston and the Hook). Rumours of an impending German landing on the low-lying coast of Little Holland may even have penetrated as far inland as the Hythe, brought there by my mother from my birthplace at Frinton on Sea (where everyone kept a bag packed with night things and a change of clothing, in the event of a sudden evacuation; but, in Colchester, this precaution was not considered necessary). But such rumours would scarcely have ruffled the walled calm and regularity of St Leonard's House and its garden, the daylight hours marked out by the gentle cooing of my grandmother's white Barbary doves, in their green dovecot at the near end of the garden. Already, by 1914, they were both so old as to be well beyond the extensive age group to find its names on rural or urban War Memorials; and it is likely that, good Victorians as they were, they regarded the great conflagration with the same disapproval, as an example of juvenile savagery and folly, as they had previously shown for the foolish war in the Transvaal. I do not really know, as I never once heard them refer to the events of 1914-18.

In this eminently reassuring continuity, they were as much protected by their physical environment and by their numerous personal entourage: Primus, the eldest son, living in, himself a sort of superior house servant (he rang the gong, ordered the menus, and made rugs); Daisy Tawell, my grandfather's niece, taken in when her parents had been killed in a carriage accident, and who only moved from her room at the top of the house to attend meals, or to expose her faded good looks and neglected linen to the gaze of the Hythe when on her 'parish work', contained in a small basket; three house servants: Ellen, the daily, Louisa, the house parlourmaid, and Elizabeth, the cook; and Mills, the groom, who, according to rumour, had taken part in the Crimean War, as by their own engrossing mutual understanding and affection which enabled them to divide the house and its functions into two clearly delineated territories. The breakfast room, at the front, was strictly masculine, the drawing-room was my grandmother's social kingdom downstairs, the dining-room was shared, the stables went by right to my grandfather. It was the same with their weekly activities: the only one shared was attendance at matins and evensong on Sundays at St Leonard's Church (the tower of which could be seen above the garden wall). Entertaining the 'Divines' to tea was my grandmother's province. And she had herself driven out by Mills, in the gig, and wearing a bonnet and veil and a black silk dress, on various charitable missions among the narrow alley-ways that lead off Hythe Hill. Her husband attended a club, went out shooting. Every September, he went to Scotland. Their lives were parallel, rather than shared, and, although they lived in the same house, for very many years, they lived in different parts of it.

St Leonard's House was the largest in the Hythe, larger than the Rectory or the brick house occupied by the manager of the gasworks. But it was near the bottom of Hythe Hill, which, as it ran down towards the Colne and the harbour, descended likewise into want, dirt, poverty, and noisy drunkenness. The two bow-windows of the house faced across the street on to two adjacent pubs, equally crowded, and with men constantly going from the one to the other; seen through the dining-room window, which had little rounds of glass, the two pubs seemed to move, like jellies, while the figures coming and going became foreshortened, as if seen in comic mirrors at a fair. From the first floor, the bow-windows commanded a clear view up and down the Hill, almost as if one were in the path of the clattering green tram. On each side of the house were two-storeyed shops – Steggles's, the grocer's, and a chandler's, and artisans' cottages. The sheer size of the house and its ornate Georgian porch might have seemed a provocation to a neighbourhood probably the poorest in Colchester. But it was not so; the house aroused respect, not rancour.

It was a large, rambling, brick place, early Georgian, four or five storeys, though 'storey' would be an over-simplification for a house that had a whole series of different grades of level and the floors and ceilings of which curved in odd ways, putting the furniture at peculiar angles: three steps down here, six steps up there, tiny corridors that screwed around, dark doors opening on to equally dark, miniature staircases, as if the house itself was constantly trying to assert its privacy and was attempting to escape from itself. It was a permanent source of amazement to me that my grandparents, who were already in their late eighties when I first became aware of their benevolent care, did not break their legs or turn their ankles in such an ill-lit maze of traps, double-doors, and musty passages. There was even a Ghost Cupboard – in fact a room over the archway connecting the house with the stables, used to store broken furniture, old curtains and covers, and rejected china, the varied debris of very many years; because it perched over a void, and because the doors at each end were very seldom opened, the room was not so much frightening as mysterious; it was rather like a tiny room over a church porch, and so I greatly enjoyed sitting in it, looking out either on to the stable-yard or on to the street; and it was especially exciting to see the gig disappear underneath, as if I were on a bridge.

Even the day-nursery, which at one time had been my father's room (a fact recalled by the presence, under the window-seat, of his sword from the Boer War, covered in oil, and wrapped up in a cloth; and, in a green tin trunk, of his green-lined white topee and his long red underpants and red vests – I asked my mother about the colour, and she told me red kept out the heat, so I supposed that all our Empire-builders wore red underneath), was on three different levels, rising to a sort of stage that commanded the bow-window, with its view on to the two pubs and the Hill. It reminded me of what I thought must have been the view from the captain's quarters in an eighteenth-century man-of-war. The bathroom, at the top of the house, overlooking the garden, was entered by three steps down-wards. The main staircase and the many minor ones all played different tunes, the floorboards in my bedroom creaked with a full range of sounds; and on the wall of the main staircase there was a long, squiggly black line, like the sluggish course of the Colne, and that had been plastered over, a split that ran from top to bottom and that dated from the great Essex Earthquake of 1884.

My grandparents spent most of their indoor lives in the half of the house that faced inwards, away from the street and onto the long walled garden. Their bedrooms and their dressing-rooms, cut off from the rest of the house by two green-baize doors, as if to insulate them from the noise of Hythe Hill, were *côté-jardin*, at night a pool of silence. So was my grandmother's drawing-room, on the ground floor. Primus too had a bedroom and a dressing-room in some mysterious corner on the garden side, in an *entresol* between the third and fourth storeys. Daisy was right at the top, in a bedroom as impenetrable as the others on the silent side, though my sister once managed to get into it, when its occupant was out, after having shot an arrow through its (rarely) open window. (Daisy was none too clean, and liked a fug.)

My grandparents, Primus, and Daisy only moved over to the street side for meals, though even these were not all held together and in the same place. At eight, my grandparents, Tim-Tom, my grandmother's cat, and, when we were staying there, my mother, sister, and I, had breakfast in the dining-room: bacon, kidneys, sausages, partridge pie (when in season) were laid out on the sideboard for the grown-ups to help themselves, having first had porridge; and there was a silver methylated egg-boiler on the table, with egg cups and spoons all round. We sat at our places, and the cat walked all over the table, given tit-bits by our grandmother. At nine, Primus had breakfast by himself in the breakfast room, a small, dark, leathery, very masculine room on the opposite side of the corridor, and sunken below street level, giving a rather murky view on to the feet, shins, and the middles of passers-by who, from inside, appeared to be headless. His lonely, but copious, meal was witnessed by a large print depicting the Tranby Croft Scandal: Tranby Croft observed my uncle, I don't think he ever observed Tranby Croft, his head well down in the steady and regularly timed absorption of a breakfast that progressed from porridge, kipper, sausage, kidney, egg and bacon, to toast and marmalade. At ten, Daisy, her hair in curlers (she only took them off on her thrice-weekly excursions out of doors on 'parish business') had her breakfast alone in the dining-room. But lunch and dinner were family meals, 'gonged' by Primus, after checking his watch with the grandfather clock, and both with the clock on the tower of St Leonard's. My grandmother had tea in her drawing-room; my sister and I were often admitted to this very elaborate ceremony, after which we would be read to (I heard there the whole of *Little Dorrit*, in every-other-day instalments, and producing, on my part, every-other-day tears). But first there would be a close inspection of our nails, faces, and clothing. Having to go to bed early (and alone, in a huge four-poster, surrounded by heavy curtains), I never discovered where my grandparents, Primus, and Daisy spent their evenings, after supper, and before going to bed (which Primus did at nine-thirty). I *think* my grandfather and his eldest son retired to the breakfast room, as it was also called the smoke room (and it certainly smelt of smoke and cigars, as well as of kipper and leather, in the morning). My grandmother presumably went off to her drawing-room; and Daisy went up to bed (where she also spent much of the day, fully clothed, smoking, and catching up on Teddy Tail of the *Daily Mail*, her only reading, apart from the Book of Common Prayer; Primus's only reading were obituaries in the *Essex County*

Standard). But, so my sister tells me – and seven years my senior, she was an earlier witness – Daisy sometimes accompanied herself on the piano in my grandmother's drawing-room.

Here then were four people, firmly fixed in their ways, their territories, their timetables, their *sorties* (in the case of my grandmother, as elaborate as rare), their activities (or, in the case of Daisy, the lack of them), long before either my sister or I came on the scene. It must have been gradually worked out, almost by touch, back in the 1890s or the 1900s, though I daresay conventions had hardened and become increasingly frozen with time. There *had* been gradual changes: according to my mother, rather a hostile witness, Daisy spent more and more time in bed and became more and more neglectful of soap. Primus had certainly become odder, more withdrawn, more taciturn, and more obsessed with checking up on the exact time, while his rug-making increased, his products gradually filling the house (my sister tells me that he made them for the whole house after first selecting the material, and that they were all quite beautifully stitched). At some previous stage, his father had ceased to address him directly, communicating only in the third person: 'Primus will wind up the clock' (not that Primus needed any telling), 'Primus will call for the library books', 'Primus will consult the glass'. Primus would address his mother as 'Mrs Ma', who, in return, called him 'Herbert dear', or 'dear Primus'; but Primus never addressed his father, and my grandmother never addressed Daisy. But my grandfather never failed to greet his niece, with a quite genuine warmth – she was his ward – when she emerged downstairs at ten, even asking her what she was going to do, though this must have been something of a formality, for he did not wait for the answer, which would generally have been 'nothing'. My mother, when present, would try to talk to everybody, thereby breaking a number of long-recognized House Rules, and causing my father – in any case very rarely present – a certain embarrassment. My mother proclaimed the need 'to draw Primus out', but out he would not be drawn, even under her direct questioning, *with*-drawing silently, with his bobbins, needles and stuff, to the breakfast room or to his fortress somewhere upstairs on the garden side (I think he too qualified for a green-baize door). Primus and my father and the middle brother, Arthur (a rare visitor, who worked in Southwold), had whispered conversations, in which there were oblique references to 'the Guv'nor', when they met on one of the many landings or dark staircases. But Primus and my father cannot have had much to say to each other, the latter having spent most of his life away from the Hythe, indeed from England, his eldest brother showing the greatest reluctance ever to absent himself from the house for more than twenty minutes, the statutory time he assigned to his twice-daily walks or to shopping. The two walks never varied: morning through the footpath past Paxman's and the lime pit, turn by the blind donkey, to the duck pond, back the same way: afternoon, to the harbour, as far as the gasworks, back the same way.

My grandparents addressed one another as 'Charlie' and 'Mrs Ma'. They even had quite long conversations about Colchester affairs, my grandmother questioning 'Charlie' about his friends 'up town', a very distant territory which exercised some fascination for her, but which she had not visited for many years. But my grandfather would avoid any topic concerned with kitchen affairs; and Mills, the stables, and the mare Jenny, would remain beyond my grandmother's enquiries or criticisms. When 'the Guv'nor' announced – as he did once or twice a month, after one of the groom's regular drinking-bouts – that Mills had been sacked, the appalling sentence would be received in silence, as would that, the next day, that he had been reinstalled and 'given another chance'. Mills certainly had had a great many 'chances' since Crimean days. The garden, on the other hand, was a recognized common topic between them, though it was also – like the interior of the house – shared out territorially, the potted geraniums and the doves the domain of the old lady, the greenhouse and orchard and the men's lavatory by the wood-shed at the far end, that of the old gentleman (my sister was given strict instructions never to play in that end of the garden), the lawn and the shrubbery, common ground. Tim-Tom, the large, and very aged – nearly twenty when he died, as if in homage to his master and mistress – black cat, who had earlier survived falling through the glass roof of the scullery, in a sudden leap from the bathroom window, frightened by the sudden shriek of the geyser, an antique, shining, brass instrument, was an interest also shared between them (as was also an equally aged Labrador, born the same day as my sister), though Tim-Tom had a special chair in the old lady's drawing-room and was rumoured to sleep in the old man's dressing-room. Tim-Tom was perhaps the only inhabitant to have the whole house as his territory, ranging from drawing-room to the kitchen, from dressing-room to dressing-room, from the dining-room table to that of the breakfast room (he attended all three breakfasts, as well as lunch and supper, *on* the table, participating in the meals, if not in the somewhat limited conversation). The 'Divines', Canon Carter, the Vicar of St Leonard's, and the Revd Gilbert Newcomen, his companion, were the special conversational concern of the old lady. Although the old man was a regular churchgoer and a churchwarden, he did not seem quite at ease with the Revd Mr Newcomen, whom he may have regarded as effeminate. I certainly found his appearance very extraordinary, for he had a red wig, which was not always on straight, wore starched frills round his clerical collar, and had rows of little buttons down his front. It is possible that my grandfather felt social concern for the 'Divines' was the proper function of the lady of the house.

My sister and I were not subjected to any of these unstated House Rules, though the former, seven years older than myself, was not only aware of them, but took a malicious pleasure in breaching them. We were both allowed to prattle away at table, often to the visible amusement of our grandparents, though neither of us ever succeeded in breaking the sombre, stony taciturnity of Primus, or the cottony daydreams of Daisy, who would, however, find animation and even voice at the sight of gooseberry jam. She had a sweet tooth, like a child of ten or so, which, in many ways, is what she had remained. I think I was too overawed by the solemnity and ceremony of these family meals – with a full display of silver tureens, cruets, and some rather mysterious objects: a silver fish with a ring through its nose, a silver swan, its feathers fanning out – to profit much from such indulgence. My sister claims that, at four or five, I was as taciturn as my uncle. But I can recall one occasion when, having come in very excited, and with the feeling of having something important to communicate, I not only spoke, but insisted on being heard by the old man, who was rather deaf. I had been out 'shopping' – or so it was called – with Mills in the gig. On the way back, coming down Clyngo Hill, Jenny had stumbled and fallen, nearly tipping us both out (I was strapped in next to Mills). I announced this, as an item of original news, in the middle of lunch: 'Gee-gee Jenny had a fall', repeating it till I was quite sure my grandfather had heard. I could see no harm in the statement, but the old man was very angry, and Mills was sacked on the spot (to be reinstated the same evening).

Before my time, when they had both been more active, my grandparents had had quite a wide circle of friends. I have seen photographs of shooting parties setting out from St Leonard's House: men with hats and extravagant moustaches, boys in caps and knickerbockers, my grandfather's white walrus moustache marking out the middle, rather like a group photograph of a college. But I can only remember one of these in my time, and that had been something of a disaster: the gig, the picnic basket, and the guns had taken up position in a clearing in the woods near Wivenhoe; suddenly a rabbit had run into the open, and, hit, had jumped into the air, to fall in a small, bloody bundle. I had cried and cried, and was never again taken on one of these expeditions. The 'Divines', as I have said, were the old lady's preserve; they came to tea on Sundays, she went to tea at the Vicarage on Thursdays, Louisa's afternoon off. Sometimes my sister and I were taken, to the embarrassment of the Revd Mr Newcomen, who shied away from children, as he did from cats, with an almost visible shudder. But if we kept very quiet and sat very still, and did not spill, we were tolerated – and Canon Carter even *liked* children – and it was all well worth the effort at extra good behaviour and being dressed in a white silk shirt and velvet knickers, white socks, and black pumps, for there was always an array of tea-cakes, crumpets, muffins, buttered toast, sandwiches of half a dozen varieties, and very finely cut, white and brown bread and butter, a variety of jams, scones, cake with caraway seeds, chocolate cake and chocolate fingers, on little tables that fitted one above the other. The 'Divines' certainly made a big thing of tea.

Then there was old Mr Pawsey, the owner of the cattle-cake factory on the harbour and who had a lot of grown-up children. I am not sure of the exact status of Mr Townsend, the manager of the gasworks (that, with the prevailing wind from the east, could be smelt from the wood-shed at the bottom of the garden). Apart from the 'Divines', he was the nearest middle-class neighbour. Though my mother disapproved, my sister and I would jump at any opportunity to go and play in the Townsends' garden, which possessed a miniature tram, painted green, and with an open top, which could be pushed up a gradient, to the buffers at the far end of its rails, and which would then run down, almost at the clattering speed of the trams that came down Hythe Hill, stopping quite gently at its terminus, which had a real platform, just as the real tram stopped at its terminus, every twenty minutes, on the corner by the harbour. Certainly, the old man had nothing against the Townsends, and the youngest son, Charlie, was his godson. At eight or nine, it was already apparent to me that my mother, who was the seventh child of a country doctor, had a more rigorous view of social relations and hierarchies than my Cobb grandparents. She even took against the miniature tram, saying that it was ostentatious and *nouveau* -something, that the Townsend children were spoilt. My grandfather had come up in business and had married well, but he was a simple, unpretentious man.

He met his fellow-Masons – he had been something important at the local Lodge, as well as at the annual Oyster Feast – at the Club, they did not come to the house. But my grandmother had a great many relations in the neighbourhood: Prested, White Colne, Halstead – the Hills were an extensive family – and these provided some of the sporting and shooting visitors. There were also regular visitors to the back door, especially in winter, with woeful tales, and generally accompanied by very ragged children, wearing old corduroy trousers, cut down to make rather long shorts, and held up by string, and with bare feet. These were always provided with small parcels of food, wood, and coal. A great many other small parcels went out into the Hythe with the gig. The old people were not blind to the extreme poverty of the neighbourhood; and 'Mrs Ma', in black silk and bonnet and veil, and Daisy, with her basket, had fixed hours and days for delivering these packets. Nor were they in the least resented by the local people. Fourteen or fifteen years after their death, visiting the Hythe while in the army, I found them still spoken of, in the numerous pubs, with that uniquely English mixture of deference and local pride (the Hythe was very much a community, on the fringes of the town, and in an area which had grown around a still active port, open not merely to barge traffic, red-sailed, and to coasters, but also to boats from Denmark, with children on deck who had tow-coloured hair, the little girls in bright smocks and with their hair in plaits, my first 'foreigners', though they did not seem so, they were so very much part of the Colne; and there was a reminder of them, too, in the little church of Copford, where there was a portion of human skin under glass, allegedly of a Danish blasphemer, who had been skinned alive at some remote time, the skin in its frame the gift of a Nathaniel Cobb in the 1770s. So, what with the Colne and the village my grandfather had come from, Denmark seemed very close), 'They were real old-fashioned people, not at all stuck up, and very kind.' 'Old Mr Cobb used to stop for a word, every day.' 'The old lady never went out without her bonnet and veil.' 'You should have seen the gig, the paint on it *shone*.' Nor, so it seemed, had they ever *preached*. My grandfather was a drinking man; and living opposite two very rowdy pubs, the red curtains of their windows throwing a reddish glow over the middle of the hill, he took drunkenness and shouting and wild bouts of singing, especially at weekends, as part of the Hythe scene. He knew about Mills's drinking habits, and as long as they caused no grave damage to the horse or to the gig, he preferred to ignore them. Drunkenness was as much a feature of the steep hill as the muffin-man with his bell at 4 p.m., the organ-grinder with his monkey, the lamp-lighter with his long pole, and the brilliantly lit trams as they careered downwards to the river. My grandparents probably knew a great deal more about their neighbours than did the 'Divines', shut away in the Vicarage, the Revd Mr Newcomen even more cut off as one of the last surviving Tractarians. It would have been hard to imagine that fastidious, bewigged, starched, frilled, manicured, and powdered High Anglican not turning up his nose in distaste when confronted with the pungent (and most appetising) smell of cattle-cake emanating from the harbour, harder still to picture him picking his way down one of the narrow, filthy alley-ways that lead off the Hill, though the bald and rotund Canon Carter was no doubt much closer to his parishioners.

I think what impressed Mrs Steggles, the greengrocer, when I talked to her in 1943, was the fact that my grandparents had been so *old*, had lived so long in the Hythe, and had made so few concessions to changing tastes and fashions. They had stuck to the brightly painted, polished gig, my grandmother to bonnet and veil, black silk, and voluminous fur, my grandfather to high-winged collar, narrow jackets buttoned down, panama, and boots. Mills too, known in every pub, regularly dismissed – one could imagine him going into one of the pubs opposite, and saying: 'the Guv'nor has sacked me again' – and as regularly forgiven – had likewise become part of a local legend, embroidered perhaps to the extent of having him fall off his box, which he never had. The 'old people' had maintained their style of living to the very end, almost as an act of defiance, more likely because they knew no other, and possibly were as much conditioned by elderly servants, as their elderly servants were held in bondage to the rigid habits and timetable of their master and mistress. They made their regular appearances at regular times, on foot, or, together with Mills, in the splendid gig. They might shut themselves away within the house, *côté-jardin*, which was the chosen realm of sleep and daytime silence (there was little sleep, even for a child, on the street side, on a Saturday) or afternoon doze; but they did not draw their blinds on to the Hythe; and any passer-by, from the raised platform offered by the right-hand pavement, as one went down the hill, could look down into the dark, cool depth of the two front rooms, lit by a flickering fire that reddened the silver. Primus, at nearly seventy, was hardly more *modern* than his parents; and there was nothing *modern* about poor Daisy, who, at fifty or more, still wore the clothes that she had possessed at nineteen, at the time of the disaster to her parents; this was not in an effort to cling to a distant girlhood, but because the pocket money her uncle gave her was either not sufficient to invest in new clothes, or, more probably, was spent on cigarettes, chocolate, and sweets. Nor had there been anything *modern* about Daisy's upbringing; there was hardly anything that she could do for herself, she could not cook or sew, nor even make her bed (which, so my mother claimed, remained unmade for weeks; it may well have been so; but my mother was a harsh judge of Daisy, seeing in her the very figure of *sloth*, something that outraged her own industry and independence, displayed already in her twenties, when she had taken up a teaching post in a Boer school in Bloemfontein; she would frequently complain that her father-in-law was over-indulgent, and that Daisy should have been put to something *useful*, though it was hard to see what that could have been); she was extremely ignorant and was quite incurious, and her only social accomplishment was to be able to play the piano and to sing (so my sister tells me, for I never heard her do either; such activities must have belonged to the hidden world of 'after bedtime' when the port came out, and my grandmother and Daisy moved over to the garden side). Daisy's father had been a country solicitor; and Daisy had been brought up like a young Victorian middle-class girl: to do nothing other than wait for marriage. By the time I came along, she had long since given up waiting for that. All she waited for now was the next meal.

The landlords of the two pubs directly opposite, the Dolphin and the Green Dragon, could have regulated their watches from the different *entrées* and *sorties* to and from St Leonard's House: Ellen, the first on the scene, at 7.30, shaking out the mat on to the street; Primus, very erect, collared-and-chained, on foot, with his stick and hat, at 10 sharp treble-checked (back at 10.20 sharp); Daisy, with basket, at 11.15 (back at 12.15, but not on the dot, she was not punctual, to change for lunch); the old man, driven up the Hill, to his club, at 3.30; Primus, out again, watch in hand, at 3.45, the second 20-minute walk, before returning to make the arrangements for his mother's tea, communicating her preferences to Louisa; the old lady, walking to the Vicarage, up the Hill, at 4 (a reminder that it was Thursday); at 6.30, the old man driven back, the gig put away, and the street entrance to the stable-yard closed, to be re-opened at 7 by Mills, on his first visit of the evening to the Dolphin, moving next door to the Green Dragon at 8.30, back to the Dolphin for an hour before closing time. Ellen would go home at 9. Nothing much would happen after that, though Mills presumably struggled back to his room over the stables at about 11.

Each of these figures was part of the landscape, indeed, *moving* figures, not static and long-legged, as in a Lowry painting; and each offered the living reassurance of continuity. Take one away, and the pack would be incomplete, so that the whole thing would break down. The old people were eighty-nine, turning ninety, and ninety-one at the time of their deaths, within six months of one another. They had lived in the house for as far back as most people could remember. They had been there at the time of the Earthquake, when my father had been still a schoolboy at the Royal Grammar and had seen a steeple fall down on his way to the Lexden Road. They had been there at the time of the Jubilee, at that of the Boer War, the death of the Queen (my grandfather used to say that he could never get used to having a King), and in 1914, and they were still there in 1918. St Leonard's House and the Hythe had been through a great many things together; and my grandfather had even provided the new bells for the church which had announced both the happier and the more sinister of these events. So it would have seemed a very long time indeed, probably as long as the unforgettable presence of the Revd Mr Newcomen, a sort of ecclesiastical *Dorian Gray*, fighting back against *les outrages du temps* under his red wig and his pomaded skin, which, close up, looked like the delta of the Bramaputra, dressed in the elaborate manner of a mid-Victorian High Churchman – although, in fact, they had only been in the house about sixty years at the time of their deaths in 1926. It was hard to say just when the Revd Mr Newcomen had turned up at the Vicarage, or what function he served there; but, again, for the Hythe, Canon Carter and the Revd Mr Newcomen, in that unchangeable order, had been like Tweedledum and Tweedledee, as far as memory went back. The Hythe seemed to favour couples and 'Charlie' and 'Mrs Ma' were a very loving, very devoted one; it was as a couple that they had thus presented the familiar reassurance of apparent permanence. It was merciful, to all concerned, that, after 'Charlie's' death, 'Mrs Ma' only lingered on for another five or six months, increasingly confused and wandering, her conversation harking back to people and places of the 1840s and 1850s, to Elizas, Prudences, Constances, and Adel-aides, to Nathaniels, Ebenezers, Hyrams, and Isaiahs, whom she now took to be familiar to all around her, about whom she reminisced in the rather quavering voice of a young girl, and who could probably have been identified from the gravestones of the churchyards at Prested and White Colne. My sister and I have heard her thus rambling on, in between bouts of tears, among dead aunts and cousins and relatives never mentioned perhaps during the previous forty or fifty years, reaching back further and further in time, even before 'Charlie', when 'Charlie' was still in Copford, and when she herself had been a tall, strong, big-limbed young woman, in a large house in Prested, Colchester a place to visit for important shopping, the Hythe unthought of, her life ahead of her. It was merciful, so the older neighbours told me, that she did not have long to wait. And then, with her death, and as if in homage to the old couple, everything began to fall apart: the house, Primus, Daisy, Mills. Whether that other couple, the two 'Divines', left the Vicarage together, or whether the one survived the other, I do not know. But that is to look ahead. My grandparents had succeeded in immobilizing a community and a quarter in a period of time, as if one year would always be like the previous one, and as if the Hythe could somehow manage to live outside public history and the public calendar of catastrophe, defeat, victory, revolution, bloodshed, civil war, sedition, envy, rancour, cruelty, and violence, as long as the old regular movements went on and the blue gig with the beautiful yellow wheels made its regular appearances. Perhaps Primus's obsession with the exact time came from an obscure awareness that, as long as a strict daily routine was adhered to, things would go on as before. That, I think, is why so many people felt attached to the old lady and the old gentleman, and why, even as late as 1943, they were still remembered with a mixture of pride, affection, and wonderment.

The continuity of life above-stairs in St Leonard's House was reflected by a similar continuity below-stairs. I have said that Mills was believed to have taken part in the Crimean War – something that is wholly possible, as he would then have been somewhere between sixteen and eighteen (he did not know his exact age, nor his place of birth). I think he must have been taken on by my grandfather in about 1890, to replace a groom called William. Ellen, the daily, had been coming since the turn of the century. Louisa, the house parlourmaid, a very good-looking, stately woman, had been engaged for seventeen years, 'walking out' with her 'young man' on Thursday afternoons (hence the tea at the 'Divines') and every other Sunday, washing and darning his socks and collars; she said that she would not leave 'the old lady' for as long as she lived and she only got married in 1927, a year after the old lady's death, when she was in her late forties and her 'young man' must have been topping fifty. I think such devotion and self-abnegation were by no means uncommon, and modern social historians would be mistaken to identify master–servant relations in stark terms of exploitation. It could not be said, for instance, that the old man exploited Mills, whose main function at least by the time I came on the scene, was to see that the mare got enough exercise to remain in good trim; both horse and gig had by then largely outlived their daily use, but, if they went, what was to become of Mills?

So they stayed, and uses – most agreeable ones for my sister and myself – were invented for all three (Jenny, Mills, and the gig). When I was very small, I was lifted up and strapped in the front, on the driver's seat, next to Mills, while my sister sat on the gun box at the rear end, facing backwards. Later, when I was considered safe, our positions were reversed; my sister thought it was grander and more dignified fo face forwards, high up above the street and little low houses, high enough to be able to look into the bedrooms of the Hythe cottages (which looked rather like the fishermen's cottages on the flat coast). It looked even as if she were driving. I preferred the back seat, just as, later, I preferred the open back platform of Paris buses, as there is more truth in the street scene as it unwinds from the back: a vantage point that catches people unawares and in the belief that they are unobserved; how often, looking backwards, as the street drew away in reverse, would I see a small child in the process of picking its nose or surreptitiously pocketing an apple from a stall; whereas, from the front, people would behave as if they were in the path of a public procession, look up, even wave, or lift their caps. As a historian, it is still the gun-box seat that I prefer, surprising as it does people in intimacy, in unconscious private gesture, hunched up, or plunged in their own thoughts, slouching, their hands in their pockets, and spitting yellowish gobs of tobacco into the gutter. Furthermore, anywhere in the Hythe, but especially on the headlong downward slope towards the river, the gig would be followed by small groups of running barefoot boys and girls, the former holding up their baggy corduroys, calling out, in strident Essex, for chocolate, sweets, or even for the core of an apple, but, oddly (by present standards), never shouting abuse at the little creature perched up facing them.

The pretext for such daily excursions, generally at about mid-morning, was shopping. And my sister can recall an earlier time when the gig had actually stopped outside the fishmonger's in Head Street, and the fishmonger, in his blue-and-white striped apron and straw hat, had actually himself *come out into the street* and handed up the fish, which was then put into the box under the seat, wrapped around in ice and leaves. Then it would stop at the toy shop, which would engulf the little girl perhaps for as much as three-quarters of an hour, leaving Mills in charge of the horse, and unable to get down, at the end of which she would emerge with a twopenny set of coloured prints, used later, up in the front, for a game of Snap with the groom. But this conventional form of shopping had almost entirely ceased in my time, to be replaced by one which seemed to me quite mysterious. Mills would first head up the hill, stopping here and there at brightly painted pictorial signs: a black bull, a volunteer, a red cow, an eagle, an eagle and child, a dragon, a lion, a bear, a castle, cross-keys, a shield, a ship, an engine, a liner, a plough, a moon, a half-moon, a sun with spikes around it, an oak tree, a man in profile wearing a funny hat, Queen Boadicea driving a chariot, a black boy, a crown. Mills would climb down, give the horse a nosebag of oats, and disappear inside. I could not make out what he *bought* in all these places, he never came out with anything, though his good humour seemed to increase with every stop, and so would the speed of our progress, so that, on the homeward downhill run, we would be going at a fair gallop, and I would hold on to the railings round the back of the box with both hands. I was long puzzled by the apparent purposelessness of these often roundabout pictorial itineraries (in the course of which it would sometimes be necessary to double back in our tracks and return to a half-moon or a queen already visited, as if Mills had forgotten something there); but as they took us all over Colchester, even into the narrow streets of the Dutch Quarter, or past long brick walls of endless barracks, or past the house with bullet-holes in it, or in front of Mr Death's, the coal merchant, as there was always something new to look at from my high perch, while Mills was inside, and as Mills himself would be whistling quite merrily after the fifth or sixth stop, I thought this type of 'shopping' very much worthwhile.

So did my sister, out in the front. But then she was more directly motivated, as these excursions were accompanied by a game that, in addition to Snap, Mills and she used to play between stops: who could think of the names of twenty public houses? Then, thirty? Or even forty? Mills always won. Once, at lunch, unguardedly, she asked our grandfather why Mills was so much better at the game than she was. It was only after the purpose of these expeditions had been explained to me that I understood the full implication of my terrible gaffe on the subject of 'gee-gee falling down'. Even so, 'shopping' went on in this way till the deaths of the old man and the old lady. Jenny *had* to be exercised. It is true that Mills was also sent out on more specific errands, would meet the old man at the North Station (very prestigious, as *North* always is), St Botolph's or the Hythe, if he had been away, or meet my mother at Hythe Halt, and would take the old lady out to the Lexden Road or to Mr Pawsey's house beyond the Clacton Road; but such missions were rare. He also took me out on foot, very early in the morning, to look for mushrooms (he called them 'rumes') in the fields around Wivenhoe Park. We nearly always came back with plenty. Mills was a man of many resources. He seemed to know the mushrooms as well as he knew a hundred-odd historical or allegorical signs. I never discovered if he were literate; but it has since occurred to me – as a result of working on late eighteenth-century French urban history – that he may have *read* his way across the town, from picture to picture, much as Parisian *commissionnaires*, laundresses, and servant girls guided themselves through the city from hanging emblem to hanging emblem: here a gigantic key, here a boot, here a yellow hat, here a flowing wig, there a vast spyglass, there a huge pair of scissors, there an inn-sign. But this is mere supposition. Ellen and Louisa could read; but Elizabeth, the cook, a tiny redhead from one of the Colnes, and who had been in service since she was nine, her parents happy to see her warm, clothed, and fed, could not. She too had been in the house for an unknown number of years, I don't think that she herself knew just how long. When my sister and I were staying in the house, coming over from Frinton, room would be found for our nannie: the first, Rose, who I think died of tuberculosis in 1916, the second Kate Scurrell, the eighth child of a country family from Great Holland, and who had somehow learnt to read and who later taught me my numbers.

For a small boy, from the rather hazy memory of three or four, to the much closer observation of eight to nine, St Leonard's House and the Hythe represented an ideal world of stability, predictability, and changelessness, as *solid*, as well-made, and as lasting as the objects on the tables or in the saddle-room, and in very marked contrast to the nomadic existence led by my parents, in between my father's periods of duty in the Sudan. St Leonard's House was *home* and safety, Primus beating the gong gave the assurance of an unruffled future. Yet the safety provided by the high-walled garden and by the up-and-down house, with its creaking floorboards, its curved ceilings and sloping floors, its huge wood-encased bath and its generous wood-encased lavatories, the pans in pink and white patterns, by my grandmother's little silver wheelbarrow, used to contain peppermint creams, and by her teacups with violets, by her Barbary doves, and by the old familiar rich smells, and the changelessness of the daily routine were likewise illusory. There was a dreadful, hideous, inadmissible occasion when I was nine and when even the peace of the walled garden and the attempt to find reassurance in several bound volumes of nineteenth-century numbers of *Punch* failed to drive away the awful memory of violence; Kate and I had been for a walk beyond the Clacton Road, and, on the way back, she had seen a crowd by the roadside, and I had followed her. There had been a motor accident, involving a bull-nosed Morris: a grey-haired woman laid out on the removed front seat, with trickles of blood running from the corners of her mouth and her nose, her face ashen, her eyes frightened and wide, a woman in a black dress with blue and yellow flowers on it – a dress that I can still see, and her shoes lying in the road, and one of her stockings coming down almost to her knee: the next day I learnt that her name was Mrs Elizabeth Knight, and that she had died in Colchester Infirmary; it was in the *Essex County Standard*, which I read surreptitiously, at a favourable moment between the first two breakfasts. I never told anyone about the accident, partly because, if I had, Kate would have been in trouble, as the Clacton Road was beyond the authorized limits of our walks – the woodyards and sawmills on the other side of the Colne and the fields near Wivenhoe Park – but mainly because the evidence of death seemed to me something so completely inadmissible that I knew that neither my mother nor my grandparents would ever be able to drive it away. I could not get the colours of the dress out of my mind, and even the doves and the walled garden were powerless. The Victorian calm had been breached by 1926; and I never felt entirely safe again.

The same year, the old people died, and Primus, at seventy, went to live in a boarding-house, The Grange, in Clacton on Sea. At first, it all turned out surprisingly well. Now he could take his two twenty-minute walks on the Pier, which might have been designed for him, timing himself, four times up and down, in his usual long-legged stride. I have a photograph of him, looking the picture of health, twirling his stick, and with a pipe in his mouth. But it did not last; he was being persecuted by two old ladies, who, he was convinced, wanted to marry him, and, worse, had designs on his gold hunter. His complaints and fears got more and more strident; in the end, my father had to go over, and have him driven from Clacton to Severall's Hospital, where he died, in less than a year, of senile dementia. It was the only time, apart from a year up the Amazon, that he had been away from home, 'Mrs Ma' having decreed, when he was twenty-one, that he was delicate. Poor Daisy was found a room in the Hythe, down an alley off the hill, with a woman who was paid to look after her, feed her, and see to her changes of clothing; but, losing all interest in life, and without her uncle to greet her in the morning, she soon took to her bed, and my father received a badly spelt letter in green ink, from the woman with whom she had been placed, to say that she had 'passed away quietly'. I am sure she did that, she had always tried not to be a nuisance; I think she died of loneliness and despair. But, as my mother said at the time: 'Where could *we* have put Daisy?' Louisa at last got married. Mills went into an old people's home and was kept in drink and tobacco by what my grandfather had left him. I believe he lived to almost a hundred. Ellen and Elizabeth got positions elsewhere. And we never went to the Hythe again, though, in 1943, when I was stationed at Dovercourt, I cycled over, visited Copford, and spent two nights in St Leonard's House, sleeping on an Army camp-bed in my old bedroom next to the Ghost Cupboard. The house had been taken over by a Signals Unit; and the garden had grown quite wild, the dovecot was still there, but the greenhouse had lost most of its glass and was falling in. One could still pick out the pattern of flower-beds, and the graves of Tim-Tom and the old Labrador were still visible as slight mounds in the thick undergrowth at the far end near the rotting wood-shed. Only 'Mrs Ma's' geraniums, in their two stone pots, had prospered.

THREE

Beyond the Hythe

OF COURSE there are bound to be many *zones d'ombre*, many questions that remain unanswered because they had never been asked in the first place, in any account provided by the often faulty recollections and perceptions of a child, however observant and retentive that child might be. Take my own case: it is clear that I must have been pretty shaky on dates, even important ones concerning my own family. When I wrote 'The House in the Hythe' some time in 1979 I even managed to grant my grandparents two extra years of life, having them both die in 1928, when in fact my grandfather died in the middle of 1926 and my grandmother at the end of that year. I remember my sense of shock, when, a couple of years later, I saw 1926 on their gravestone in Copford churchyard. I had got even that wrong! I recall my parents waking me up from a deep sleep, at a time when we were living in Cumberland Gardens Tunbridge Wells, in order to show me a beautiful golden coach – a model in shining metal – of the one used by the incoming Lord Mayor of London; they had been up to the Empire Exhibition at Wembley and had brought back this present for me; but I have no idea just what year that could have been. My concern for dates came much later and was related much more to the facts of public life than to anything that might have concerned me personally. Some dates will stand out, of course: 1939, 1940, 1944, 1945, for they are both public and private, the points at which the two overlap, generally with dreadful consequences to the private individual. But these are likely to be followed by decades that just have names: the sixties, the seventies, without a clearer identity. Equally, as a child, whether in Colchester or in Tunbridge Wells, I would not have attached any particular significance to the twenties,

54

would not have sought to remind myself: 'I am now living in the twenties', though, for some reason, the thirties would achieve a much more positive identity, no doubt due to the fact that they were heavily marked out by a *negative* element of the greatest importance: that, for much of the year, I was *not* living at home, though of course there would be the greatest possible difference between being a boarder at a prep school or a public one, being an undergraduate at Oxford, or living much of the year in Paris. Dates are better signposts to guide us through public events, or even through the obscurity of other peoples' lives than as a measurement to our own personal experiences.

What will a child be likely to notice? And what will probably leave him unconcerned? Certainly, living in St Leonard's House, my bedroom facing onto Hythe Hill, I could not help being vaguely aware of the fact of drunkenness – though I might not have identified it as such – simply because the two pubs, the Dolphin and the Green Dragon were, in my direct line of vision exactly opposite on the other side of the street. There was just rather a lot of noise, the sound of laughter, quite often of singing, and the noise seemed to increase in volume as I started to doze off into a deep sleep behind the closed curtains of the huge four-poster bed. The noise didn't worry me at all; on the contrary, I came to expect it, as a sort of prelude to the gentle coming of sleep. There was nothing threatening about it, it was just part of the familiar urban scene, like the lights thrown by the trams on the ceiling. On the other hand, the presence, beyond the locked side door of the room, of the silent Ghost Cupboard, the room over the arch, caused me real fright. The door was always locked, but the silence from the other side seemed to fill my bedroom with the presence of an invisible, but waiting threat. Silence was much more frightening than noise, which simply indicated that there were people about, people who might be rough and ill-spoken, but whom I knew would be friendly. The bright lights coming through the red curtains of the two bars opposite indeed seemed a protection.

But a child would not be likely to take in the disparities of education, save as one of the more obviously unpleasant facts – the penalty of childhood – of being a child: the disagreeable obligation of having to attend school or of being exposed, for the first time, to the more obvious dangers of collectivity: the noise, the smell, the keen and cruel observation of other little boys, the first exposure to the perils of the crowd. And so a child would early acquire a sense of the future as of a time when one would be released from the tyranny of school, and so one eagerly to be looked forward to, the great release, the longed-for luxury of being alone, above all, of sleeping alone.

But, on the general subject of education, or the lack of it, as it may have applied to the case of my father and his two brothers, I had no views at all. I had never given the matter a thought. Why should I have? I knew merely that, on the day of the great Earthquake, my father had walked as usual all the way uphill from the Hythe to the area of the Lexden Road, that he had seen a church steeple fall down into the road, and that a great gap had suddenly opened up, almost at his feet, in the lawn outside the Grammar School. I think that must have been about the only time that my father had ever mentioned his school.

I don't suppose my grandfather had ever had much of an education, I don't even know at what stage he had left Copford to come to Colchester. He may have attended just the village school. But he had, at some stage – long before my time, back I suppose in the eighties or the nineties – become a comparatively rich man; and he certainly seems to have indulged in most of the tastes and display concomitant with moderate wealth: the annual grouse moor in Scotland, a gig and a horse, if not a pair (though there may have been a pair earlier on), a groom, a club somewhere up the far end of the town – a necessity as much as an indulgence for a man in business – well away from the Hythe, a generous domestic establishment, a widening network of charity locally distributed that was meant for what it was and that had nothing to do with status. My grandparents were far too self-assured to have been even *aware* of status, it was not the sort of thing that they would have bothered about. They had long grown accustomed to a certain degree of wealth and would not have felt the need to question what must have seemed to them their rightful position in a society which had been set within fairly narrow geographical limits. They had every reason to have felt altogether content with their fate, which had many of the markings of a pretty conventional Victorian success story. Had they not come up by dint of hard work, careful saving and a delicately balanced combination of prudence and the ability to take risks? They had no doubt also been lucky, or well advised, in their investments. Anyhow, they lived – and moved: the gig must have been out most days, save Sundays, for much longer than it was ever in the stables – very comfortably within a well-defined circle of relatives and close friends, spreading from the Hythe, Ardleigh and Wivenhoe, to Prested Hall, Kelvedon, Tiptree, Marks Tey, Earls Colne and White Colne and Hadleigh. There may even have been one or two outposts in the neighbouring county to the north, though I think this is doubtful: the Stour seems as much a frontier as the Blackwater certainly was to the south. I don't know whether they were often in the habit of visiting Copford, though later they were to be buried there. I would surmise that perhaps my grandfather felt that he had done well to have left Copford behind him; and his brother, or brothers, seem to have been equally disinclined to return as it were to roots. Copford may not have had altogether happy memories. What strikes me now is the narrowness of the area in which they moved, whether it was a matter of seeking a bride, or of visiting relatives and friends. My grandfather had his annual visit to Scotland, his twice yearly visits to Brussels, and I suppose monthly visits to London. My grandmother seems always to have been reluctant to move beyond the bounds of a clearly defined area of North Essex. I don't think she had ever been to London, Chelmsford was well beyond the limits of her territorial imagination. When their second son took up work at a brewery in Southwold, I imagine they must have visited him, his wife and their two grandchildren there; and they might very occasionally descend on us in Frinton. At some stage, too, – the almost immobile Primus must have got in a visit to Clacton: given his adherence to a strict and changeless routine, I cannot believe he would have risked such a bold jump in the dark when he opted for the Grange boarding-house – once the old people had died. But, as I have said, in general, their sociability was firmly confined to North Essex.

Of course, some of such unquestioning self-confidence may have been imported from the Hills side of the family, something even suggested by the fact that Hills was the second name given to my father at birth. It looked very much as if my grandfather, and possibly at least one of his brothers – may have, married upwards, though, mercifully, I would never have entertained such rather carping notions at the time. Upward mobility is not a concept that would have been even vaguely perceived by an affectionate child who revered both his grandparents because they were so old, had lived so long, were so kind and so indulgent (I was the youngest, by as much as six or seven years, of their four grandchildren). For me, who had only known them in their eighties, they had always been venerable, my grandfather had always had an enormous, drooping white moustache, my grand-mother had always worn a bonnet and a veil. How could I ever have thought of either of them in their perhaps struggling thirties, their more confident forties or fifties? Upward mobility is an ugly phrase born of a much more questioning, more envious age. But, looking back from my own relative old age, over the huge gap of sixty years, the Hills do seem to have been pretty grand people, with a grand address: Prested Hall, now a fairly extensive ruin standing forlornly in a field, had been a big, eighteenth century brick and plaster place. Henry Hills, my grandmother's brother, was described at the time of her death, as a famous sportsman, horseman and shot, quite a local figure, appar-ently known throughout the northern part of the County (I don't know whether any of them had been more than vaguely aware that it had a *southern* part, too). My Great-Uncle Henry was also some sort of a Captain. He lived in considerable style in Earls Colne and possessed a very early motor-car. If my sister is right in thinking that Charlie and his brother (Alfred?) had married sisters, both from the Hall, it looks very much as if that generation of Cobbs were in the process of hauling themselves up not just through hard work and business acumen, but also as a result of socially prestigious marriages that opened up to them some of the bigger houses of North Essex. Copford is only a few miles from Colchester, but, socially, these two brothers at least – and, I suppose at much the same time, one of their sisters had married into the Marsh family, of Overshot Mill, Earls Colne – seem to have come a long way up from wherever they had started from in the village. My father, who, unlike my mother, was the very reverse of a snob, and who no doubt liked to romanticize about the humble origins of his paternal forbears, once wrote to me that they had all come from a long line of peasants. This would have been putting it much too low, I don't think there were any peasants in Copford. I have the will of Nathaniel Cobb, who died in 1830; he owned a cottage and several acres of land that he farmed; he was also the village carpenter. Still, in 1864, at the time of the birth of Primus, on the birth certificate his father, then aged twenty-seven –his mother then would have been twenty-eight – is described as 'a banker's clerk', living at Abbeygate Terrace, Abbeygate Street. It doesn't sound much of an address, especially the Terrace bit.

Well, he had come a long way since then, even if the marriage had given him an advantageous start. At some stage, he had moved to the big house in the Hythe, had become a director of Moy's (a prosperous firm that imported Belgian coal), a leading figure in the local masonic community, and a churchwarden. He could certainly hold his own with the numerous Hills and Marshes, the three families getting on well together and frequently visiting one another, for shooting parties, elaborate meals, and festive occasions. My grandparents also had very friendly relations with two of the local dynasties: the Pawseys and the Marriages. So, long before my mother first met her in-laws – in 1908 or 1909 – my Cobb grandparents had established themselves as the leading family in the Hythe, then not quite such a rundown area as it has since become, though then containing pockets of extreme poverty and a number of plague spots approached down suppurating closed alleys. I think they had chosen the Hythe for the convenience it offered by its proximity to Moy's, or the house may have gone with the job. It was a relatively big house, something that they needed. Their marriage seems to have been a very happy one in every respect, the two were devoted to one another, but the size of the house allowed their devotion not to become too obtrusive. Each held to his or her own areas of territory, and for much of the day they went their own ways, on quite separate activities. By 1870, when my father Francis, was born, they had three sons, Primus then aged six, John Arthur, two or three. Up to the time of their death, Primus occupied his own enclave somewhere upstairs. I don't know at what stage Daisy had been taken in.

What, very much in retrospect – for it was a matter to which I would not have given any thought at eight or nine, and I was certainly right then not to have asked all these questions and to have left the old couple and their household in the secure peace of total acceptance – what surprises me most now, given their fairly generous style of living and entertaining, and the extent of their charity, both weekly and seasonal, is that my Cobb grandparents – in such marked contrast to my mother's people, one of my aunts, Mabel Swindale, being one of the earliest inmates of Girton College (she went there in 1893, at eighteen), my uncles Jack and Vernon being sent, as a matter of course and without any opportunity to question the decision regarding both their education and their future occupation, first to Epsom, then on to the Middlesex – should have apparently set so little store by education as a means of getting a good start in life. It may have been that my grandfather had never given the matter very much thought, possibly as a result of having himself had few educational opportunities, or possibly, too, with the prejudices of a self-made man: 'I left school at fourteen, and look where I am now', and that sort of thing. Not that my grandfather could ever have been described as a philistine. Like my maternal grandfather, the doctor, he had an enormous respect for Gladstone, because of his learning, and he had made a point of attending all of Dickens's public readings up in the Corn Exchange, and I think he was quite well read. My grandmother certainly was. But, so it seems, the possible advantages offered by higher education, the need to acquire technical qualifications from one of the degree-giving professional institutions so as to have the right letters after one's name, the importance of Universities were all matters that had simply passed my grandfather by.

It must have been due to a lack of imagination, it would certainly not have had anything to do with the desire to avoid what he might have considered unnecessary expense. For he was a most generous man: he came to the rescue of his second son, Arthur, in order to give him a fresh start and set him up in a job, running a boarding-house in Folkestone, which, if pretty unglamorous, very uncertain, and socially rather demeaning – I am not surprised that my mother should throughout her life have concealed from my sister and myself this particular item of family history – at least had the advantage of taking less of a toll on a health already seriously impaired than working in the steamy atmosphere of a brewery. I imagine, too, that he moved mostly in circles in which education was never discussed: polytechnics, technical colleges, professional institutions, medical schools would hardly have formed the subject of conversation at shooting parties, on the grouse moor, or over port, though, masons generally being ambitious for their children – I imagine this is one of the reasons, apart from a delight in dressing up and indulging in an exotic ceremonial, for becoming a mason – such matters must sometimes have come up at meetings of the Lodge. For my grandfather I can only surmise universities were places to which young men went, either to train for the ministry, or to idle away their nights and days in dissipation. In any case, there was then no university in North Essex or anywhere near it. I don't think he would have been very much entertained by the knowledge that, some forty years after his death, a university should have sprung up – literally – almost on his doorstep, in his favourite shooting grounds of Wivenhoe Park.

There had, it is true, been the brief, half-hearted experiment with Felsted, a school that had at least to recommend it in my grand-parents' eyes the fact that it was well within the sacred circle of North Essex; but Primus had been miserable there, and my grandmother had insisted on having her eldest back home. He had gone up the hill to the Royal Grammar, and his two brothers had followed him there, though I have no idea with what distinction, or lack of distinction. I know nothing of their showing as schoolboys, though records of marks, class lists and school reports no doubt still exist. I do not feel impelled to carry my enquiries as far as to consult them. I daresay the Royal Grammar offered quite a solid education. My father seems to have acquired an early taste for reading, a firm, clear handwriting and an ability to do simple sums; and he may have formed there a lifelong enthusiasm for rowing – throughout the first thirty years of his life, there would always be a river invitingly available to him and his clerical, stripe-jerseyed companions: first, the Colne, then the Nene, quite wide, and not so wide, little more than a trickle, almost as if he had opted for these towns because of their welcoming presence – for skating (the winters seem to have been so very much colder during my father's youth and adolescence than in mine), cricket and football. But both Latin and French seem to have left him quite untouched later in life. He had a very English attitude towards foreign languages, though while in the Sudan he acquired a smattering of Arabic.

But then, as far as I can make out, nothing much had followed in terms of training. I don't think Primus ever *had* any formal technical training as a marine engineer, save for the year – as unhappy as, and even more disastrous than, the term away at Felsted – spent crossing the Atlantic both ways and the long trip up and down the Amazon. He must have acquired a few rudimentary qualifications to have been taken on, as some sort of temporary engineer, at Paxman's Works during the First World War. They may too have been desperately short-handed and to have been only too happy to take on someone, however little skilled and already in his fifties, who lived just over the wall. It was his only other pretty brief excursion into the wider world of labour: not a very distant world. The end of the War would mean for him the return to his normal domestic activities: shopping, the menu, the laying of the table, the ringing of the gong, rug-making and seeing to the curtains.

With Primus back home, clearly for good, well-entrenched in his enclave upstairs, and with his minutely-timed appearances down-stairs, in the dining-room and the breakfast-room, there cannot have been much question of his two younger brothers being allowed to imitate him and to linger on in the house, once they had left school. Primus had managed firmly to establish his rights as first-born. For one thing there cannot have been much room for them: in my own time, my parents, my sister and I, as well as Kate, had to alternate with my Uncle Arthur, his wife, and my cousins, Ken and Marjorie – I expect that they, too, had a nannie in tow, – so that, over a number of years, we never actually *met*, they had always just left when we arrived, or we were on the point of leaving, to make way for their arrival: a simple fact of logistics that had eluded me as a child and that was only brought home to me very recently by my surviving cousin. And my grandparents were no doubt – and one could see their point of view – unwilling to run to a household which, in addition to the kitchen staff and Mills, included three strapping young Marthas. Arthur seems to have gone pretty well straight from school into the brewery at Southwold, a place beyond the safe confines of North Essex. I don't know what can have dictated either the choice of such a distant place of exile, quite unreachable in the gig (my grandparents, no doubt reluctantly, in the case of my grand-mother, who never shook off a deep suspicion of that form of transport, soon formed the habit of going there by train in order to visit their two grandchildren: Frinton at least had the advantage, from their point of view, of being manageable by gig), or of that profession. There would have been nothing against it as such: my grandparents were drinking people, and, living for much of their lives directly opposite two well-frequented pubs, they would have been very much aware of the importance of beer as a social link binding together a well-defined masculine urban community. Indeed, the evidence of their eyes and their ears must have convinced them that there was money in brewing. I expect my grandfather knew someone in the trade – probably a fellow-Mason – who had agreed to take on the young man and to train him in the essentials. Arthur may have been delicate before he ever went to Southwold; but it seems certain that the years in the brewery must have precipitated the tubercular condition that eventually necessitated the move to Folkestone – a move accountable to the current medical ethos that, at much the same time, caused prep schools to congregate in places like Seaford and Bexhill – and the acquisition of the seaside boarding-house, an episode that lends to the undistinguished and reassuringly banal history of that side of my family some of the qualities of an Arnold Bennett novel. I suppose that the actual running of the boarding-house fell the most heavily on his wife and on his daughter, leaving Arthur free to sit out on the front. The move may have prolonged his life by a few years, but he was the first of the family to die, long before his parents and his brothers, I think only in his early fifties.

His death left his children, my cousins Ken and Marjorie, with equally blighted educational opportunities. Their father, no doubt with his own experience in mind, had been anxious to do better by his son and daughter than his parents had done by him, and Ken had been encouraged to think in terms of the long, slow haul of a hospital training that would eventually allow him to qualify as a doctor. St Thomas's had been recommended. But, once his father had died – and the boarding-house does not seem to have brought in very much money – my cousin Ken, then in his early twenties, had had to take the first thing that had been going in order to earn a living as soon as possible. He had had a brief training at a London technical school that had enabled him to obtain in a short time the minimum qualifications as an electrical engineer. He had spent the whole of his subsequent working career – he died in his eighties – working, in some advisory and mostly bureaucratic capacity, for the old London County Council. I don't think that he ever found much satisfaction in his work; but he seems to have enjoyed his leisure. Unlike his father, he never *made* any beer, but he consumed a great deal of it, having his own recognised corners in a couple of pubs in Claygate, Surrey. There had been a welcome interlude between domestic life on the southern periphery of London during the Second World War which he had spent serving on a destroyer as an electrical engineer officer in the RNVR.

However, all had not been quite lost in what had looked like a wilderness of blighted expectations. These, this time no longer blighted, had merely jumped a generation. Ken's second son, whether or not with his father's active encouragement, had embarked on a medical career which took him, in due course, to a University lectureship in a specialised branch of medicine and consultancies in a teaching hospital and in a private clinic. His aunt, my cousin Marjorie, had had to leave school early, the boarding- house had been sold (I think at a loss) and she had had to fall back on something only vaguely genteel and just about on the right side of the socially proper, like learning how to arrange flowers. She had learnt how to at a college of domestic science somewhere in Central London. I think it was the same college to which my sister, exactly the same age as Marjorie, had been sent, at much the same time, to learn how to teach cooking and domestic hygiene. Flowers seem to have been a good deal more profitable than seaside boarding-houses. They had brought her three husbands, the first one for a time resident in Frant Road – on the face of it a good address – Tunbridge Wells (my mother must have often felt, with dismay, that she was being pursued by the socially less acceptable members of her husband's family and that they were closing in on her: first, there had been the boarding- house at Folkestone, and now she was being exposed to the demeaning proximity of a florist niece, in other words, a niece in trade. There was some small consolation in the fact that she was married, however unsuitably – my mother had very strict standards of suitability as far as husbands, potential or established, were concerned – for she would not be readily identified as a Cobb. But she must have been considerably relieved when Marjorie moved on to a second husband and to Canada). She had outlived a third husband, before settling in a house on an island off Vancouver.

According to my sister, a reliable authority in family matters, Henry Hills and his brother-in-law, Bobby Marsh, the owner of Overshot, had both been trained as engineers and had, at some stage, invented and then patented a gun, presumably an artillery piece, which had been adopted, some years before the outbreak of the First World War, by the War Office. This certainly had all the ingredients of a Victorian or Edwardian success story, and the lethal gun may have been one of the sources of the visibly comfortable style of life of the two of them. The success of the gun, as well as his brother-in-law's unchallenged social prominence in the county (or in the part of it that mattered), may also have been the reason why my grandfather, I imagine something of a martinet in his younger days, should apparently always have been so ready to defer to the superior professional judgment and to the greater worldly experience of the eldest brother of Catharine Hills. Anyhow, there must have been some sort of engineering tradition – and perhaps the belief that there was a great deal of money to be made in all branches of the profession – in my grandparents' close family circle. I don't know just who had plunged for Marine Engineering as a suitable vocation for poor Primus, so deft, as it very soon turned out, with needle and thread, loom and Singer sewing-machine. The choice had, it must be said, not shown very much judgment. Primus, at least, got his way. He even earned the rather grudging approval of my mother, so critical of the choice of careers made by some other members of the Cobb family, as a man of leisure. She was less approving of Daisy, who was, after all, a woman of leisure.

What I do know is that my father, six years junior to Primus, and two years junior to the no doubt reluctant brewer, Arthur (born in 1868), when his turn had come round, shortly after leaving school, had been pushed into civil engineering, without ever having been given the opportunity of undergoing a proper training that would have enabled him at least to have put a few letters behind his name. My father had wanted to train as an architect: his surviving sketches, most of them of country churches in Essex, Suffolk, Kent and Sussex – another of his unfulfilled ambitions, but one that came a good deal later in life, after his return from the Sudan, was to have been ordained as a clergyman in the Church of England – have about them an architect's firmness of line, stiffness and fidelity to minute detail; he had a deft hand at Norman cushion caps and arches in chevron patterns. I suppose this ambition had been overruled because the training would have been too long and too expensive. It was yet another example of my grandfather's shortsightedness – one would be tempted to say stinginess, had he not been so generous in other ways – but perhaps he just did not think that a long period of professional training was something worth investing in. In any case, the third son was sent off to Peterborough, to work, for the next ten years or so – he would have been twenty in 1890 – with a firm of civil engineers, Shipley-Ellis. As he was unable to afford a partnership, he stood little chance of promotion, and was only saved from vegetating for the rest of his working life in a dead-end job in this sleepy little cathedral town by the almost providential outbreak of the Boer War. The war over, he returned briefly to Peterborough with the company that he had formed from among his clerks: two corporals and nineteen sappers ('Lieutenant Cobb's company' as it was called, in a boisterous report of the proceedings in the *Peterborough Advertiser* under the headline: 'Bells, Bands, Volleys, Cheers') to receive a civic reception from the Mayor and the authorities, followed by a Thanksgiving Service at the parish church. Once the ceremonies were over, he returned, *sans trompettes ni fanfares*, to South Africa, to work on reconstruction. Despite the warmth of his reception and his brief triumph, I think he must have been very glad to have got clear of Peterborough, though, on all his leaves over in England, he would look up his friends among the clergy and the engineers there.

My father was not a man to complain, and, in any case, he would never have complained to his children. But that he did feel all his life a certain bitterness at what he must have regarded as a skimped education and lost professional opportunities was made clear to me, after his death, by my mother. He had, she told me, never had a proper training as a civil engineer and had in consequence never been a very good one: bridges that he had designed tended to fall down. (My mother took a rather dramatic view of what was no doubt a pretty humdrum profession, and, certainly, in the course of the war, all the railway bridges that my father had put up on the line from

Cape Town to Bloemfontein seem to have stood up well to the strain put on them by the numerous troop and armoured trains that went back and forth that way). He had wanted, she would go on, to do better by his children than his father had done by his brother and himself. This was why, at considerable sacrifice to his wife and to himself – they had never been able to afford a car, though this did not seem to me a very great deprivation – (I was not impressed by the sacrifice bit) he had insisted on sending my sister as a boarder to the Godolphin and myself to a prep school and to Shrewsbury. My sister and I had been a good deal luckier than our cousins, Ken and Marjorie; and, in my case, Shrewsbury would lead me on to Oxford.

On the face of it, there might be something indecent in thus subjecting my grandfather – I have tended to leave my grandmother out of it, in the belief that she had little hand in affecting decisions concerning the education of her sons – sixty years after his death, to the close scrutiny of a series of enquiries, however tentative, into what may have been his motives with regard to the education of his three sons, or indeed, what sort of a father he may have been to them. Perhaps such questioning, a bit in the nature of a cross-examination, over such a very long lapse of time, may in any case be futile, as well as irreverent, and so a bit distasteful. For there is no one about who might be able to provide any sort of answer. And, of course, at the time, one would not have expected a nine year-old boy, who revered his grandparents because they were kind to him and because they seemed to go such a very long way back in time – at nine, I had not yet decided that I wanted to be a historian, that came three years later, after reading *The Rise of the Dutch Republic*, but already the past held me in fascinated curiosity, and my grandparents provided me with a visible measurement of the passage of time – ever to have given a passing thought to such matters. I would have been a little monster if I had. These were things for grown-ups to ponder. A grandson – a son at one remove – will not have the same view of a grandparent as a son might have done. I never heard my father discuss the old people, though my mother often did, always in most affectionate terms, so I have no idea what he thought of them, more important, what he had thought of them as a young man on the point of embarking on a career that had not been one of his own choice.

How had my father reacted to a career that had apparently been imposed upon him? Had there been the ripples of a post-adolescent revolt? Had he ever tried to line up with his nearest brother, Arthur, similarly disposed of without any apparent right of reply or objection? Had some of those clergymen, in Peterborough and in Northampton, some of them still alive in my childhood, and to whom he seemed to have turned so readily for advice, provided a substitute for a father who may have been a little distant, a little unfeeling, even a bit unimaginative? There is no means of knowing, there never was as far as I was concerned, it was not the sort of question that I could have put to my father on one of our long country walks (when we discussed what we could see around us, he was a very observant man visually, knew the names of all the wildflowers and all the plants, would identify a Norman arch or an Early English pillar or a Perpendicular window: as I have said, he tended to romanticize both about a rural family and about life in the country) and he died when I was a bit over seventeen, that is at a time when he would have been disinclined to confide in a son who was still only a teenager and of whom, once I had gone to Shrewsbury, he was perhaps a little shy (and I did not try to pull aside the curtain of his shyness). Where he most revealed himself was in his stated ambitions for my sister and myself, in the most conventional feminine and masculine terms, and in which we must both have provided him with a considerable measure of disappointment: in my own case, success in the manlier sports, and a pious disposition, whether High or Low (that would not have mattered, I don't think he had very much time for the forms of worship, it was the piety that mattered). Piety was not my strong suit, and my natural, and I think very healthy, irreverence, my proneness to doubt, drew me much closer to my two medical uncles, my mother's brothers, born scoffers, lifelong mockers of the pompous, the conventional and the ambitious, than to my father, so unquestioning in most of his public attitudes, though his innate simplicity and a sort of primitive, almost boyish, egalitarianism preserved him from any hint of snobbery. Indeed, I think he would have positively rejoiced in the story of the seaside boarding-house. His total *lack* of snobbery was a further barrier between us; I was perhaps not *quite* such a snob as my mother, but I shared most of her attitudes. My father was keen on youth clubs and energetic Christian missions to the young men of the urban poor. I found such places sweaty and smelly and would not have known how to communicate with a working-class lad of my own age. Snobbery was safer, it insulated me from the unknown.

My father's literary tastes might have revealed a bit more of him to me, had I been prepared to listen: Gilbert White, Kipling, and Conrad occupied the high places in his somewhat restricted pantheon (which, however, as I recently discovered, rather to my surprise, looking through some of his books, also took in Mrs Gaskell, his copy of *Cousin Phillis* has on the title page: 'F. H. Cobb, Khartoum, July, 1922'; so my father's range may have been greater than I had imagined). Sermons, too, had a corner; but they had to be simple, straightforward, and simply expressed, he had no taste for the convolutions of theological argument. Hardy was a bit of a borderline case; on the credit side was the fact that he wrote well about the countryside and about village life – there was something very homespun about my father's tastes, it may have had something to do with the period in which he had grown up. I don't think he had ever walked in Dorset, but he had done both the North and the South Downs from end to end on foot. On the other hand, Hardy was far from sound on sex. I was told that I was too young to try him, so, of course, I did, even to the extent of enjoying his mawkish gloom. Apart from Gilbert White, the whole of the eighteenth century appeared to have passed him by. I expect it was just as well.

So I missed my chance. Between the ages of twelve and seventeen I grew increasingly distant from my father, going much the same way as my sister had travelled a few years earlier. I liked to think of myself as a Swindale, and, with my sharp, foxlike face, I certainly looked more like my mother's people than I did any of the Cobbs. Sometimes I even wondered why my mother had married a man who seemed a bit stupid. It is a familiar story, hardly worth retelling. But, over fifty years after his death, I have come to regret the barriers, some erected by myself, others by his combination of shyness and directness – there was nothing devious about him, everything devious about me,

deviousness having been my favoured armour ever since early childhood – that kept us at such a distance and that prevented me, at the
time, from learning more about his own adolescence and his no doubt
frustrated ambitions. 'Mrs Ma' and 'The Guv'nor' were probably
little more than code words, expressive no doubt of a mixture of
genuine affection and respect. But how was I, at nine, to probe behind
the simplicities of a nickname? How was I, at fifteen or sixteen, to
sound out my father on the subject of the white-moustached Charlie?

There was nothing exceptional about my father's family – my
mother's was a very different kettle of fish – and this is perhaps what
provides it with some general interest. Of course, most people are
likely to show some interest in the history of their own families, even
if it is only in order to rebuild a family tree that will enable them to
grope their uncertain way back over several generations; and this is
both natural, and, I suppose, in a way commendable. But also one
knows *more* about one's own family, the scrutiny is that much closer,
whether in terms of affection or sheer dislike, so it must provide a
better illustration of a given period than one arbitrarily chosen
whether for its fame and eminence, its villainy, its disasters, or its
eccentricities (there was certainly no lack of these in St Leonard's
House). In its sheer banality, in its intense and guarded provincialism, in its relative insignificance, it can no doubt witness for a great
many others as a chronicle of modest success, at least in the more
obvious material terms, as far as the first generation is concerned, the
point at which I came in. At the next, it illustrates both a relative
decline, and a whole series of unexpected twists and turns, some of
them imposed by outside and very public events: wars and that sort
of thing. I have even attempted to carry the chronicle through to a
third generation. I would not try to make too many claims for it, at
any of the three levels. As I have said at the beginning, there are many
zones d'ombres that cannot be penetrated. Perhaps this is just as well;
one does not want to know *all* the *secrets du boudoir*, and there is
something slightly obscene – though I am much given to it myself – in
rifling through the contents of bedroom drawers. At best, from the
immense disadvantage of a huge gap in time – almost two hundred
years – one can ask a few tentative questions and even propose a few
modest answers. My great-grandfather, Alfred Cobb, was born in

1792 – a terrible year in public history – so he was in his mid-forties when Charlie was born. My youngest son, William Cobb, now aged seven, was born in 1980, on Good Friday; his cousin, Daisy Cobb, was born one day earlier, in the same year. I have merely attempted to provide a rough-and-ready guide wire from the time of the terrible French Revolution to the eighth decade of the twentieth century. Alfred marks out a very dim, mainly undiscoverable past, William and Daisy represent the unknowable fortunes and misfortunes of a distant future. The attempt to link the two seems to me worthwhile. But then I have a vested interest as a historian.

Finally, a word about the two 'Divines'. Henry Frederick Victor Carter and Gilbert Arthur Newcomen had both attended the Canon School, Lincoln, and had been ordained in 1886 by Bishop Mitchinson. Canon Carter had been rector, first of Kettering, then of Hornchurch, followed by Brentwood, before being appointed to the Balliol living of St Leonard's, the Hythe, in 1896. In all these livings, the Revd Newcomen had acted as his unpaid assistant. The two of them spent thirty-eight years at St Leonard's, retiring in 1934. Canon Carter had died shortly after that date, and from 1934 till his own death in August 1952, the Revd Newcomen had lived at 66 Barrack Street, Colchester, an address not particularly prestigious. So the Revd Newcomen had survived his friend by over eighteen years, living to the considerable age of eighty-nine or ninety.

Ronnie Blythe, in a letter to me, had this to say about the Revd Newcomen: ' . . . Among the various things I heard at the time [of his death] was that Newcomen was Lady Londonderry's nephew, that he had sacrificed his own advancement so as to stay with Canon Carter, and that he had known Walter Pater. He wore a red wig and was (I was told) carefully made up, but these things would not have been apparent to me, had I not been informed of them. Both clergymen were respected and loved in the Hythe for their goodness and kindness . . .

'One thing I remember is that he [Newcomen] used to enquire in the local library for "something by Miss Braddon" (Mary Braddon, author of *Lady Audeley's Secret*). Bernard Shaw said of her, "she is what we now call low-brow, but her style would over-awe us now as classical". I was just a lad he saw in the library – when he was about ninety, or so they said . . .' He goes on to tell me that Newcomen had put his hand through his abundant curly hair, remarking on what a very fine head of hair he had, and taking him for a glass of sherry in the lounge bar of the Red Lion.

John Bensusan-Butt has written, on the subject of the sale of the effects of the late Revd Newcomen, in September 1952, 'I bought oil painting by Olive Newcomen, 1863, of a Donkey, head and shoulders . . . labelled on back "Sheepdog" Mrs Olive Newcomen, 20 Ovington Square, London SW. Splendid picture that I lent to the *Minories* when it became an art gallery . . . She had eight pictures in the Royal Academy 1866–1872 . . .' The immediate mourners at Newcomen's funeral were Mrs K. Quinn, Mrs N. Hooper, Miss Davies, Nurse China, and Messrs Canham and Oxley'. He is buried at Greenstead, next to Canon Carter.

There is something splendidly inconsequential about the portrait of the Donkey-Sheepdog, Head and Shoulders. It somehow goes with this bizarre, kindly man. The portrait must have dated from just about a year before Gilbert Arthur's birth.

So he seems to have retained into extreme old age the appearance I had seen through my nine year-old eyes. The red wig had presumably gone on all through those years, though it may have been replaced. I am surprised that, at sixteen or seventeen, Ronnie Blythe had not noticed it, for it is very evident in the photograph taken c. 1930, at a time when the two 'Divines' were still living at St Leonard's Rectory. It is clear, however, from what Ronnie has written, that I completely misjudged the fastidious Revd Newcomen when I suggested, in 'The House on the Hythe', that he would have been reluctant to visit some of his poorer parishioners who were living down those filthy alley-ways that led off Hythe Hill. Both 'Divines' seem to have been very dedicated parish priests.

St Leonard's Church was made redundant in 1983 and has been closed these last five years, after having for a time served the needs – surely not very extensive – of the local Greek Orthodox community, a touch of exoticism that might possibly have appealed to the Revd Gilbert Newcomen. The bells given to the church by my grandfather will no longer be heard down Hythe Hill. I find that sad, but it is an outcome that would no doubt have pleased my grandmother.

FOUR

Uncles and Aunts

Vernon and Honorine

MY TWO medical uncles, my mother's only brothers, seem both to have been somewhat reluctant doctors, though I have no idea what in fact each would have preferred to have become. They had been pushed into medicine by their father, my maternal grandfather, James Swindale, who, judging from the photograph in a silver frame that used to be prominently displayed, like a medical ikon, on my mother's dressing-table, was an impressive, bearded figure, a country doctor in Binfield, a Berkshire village not far from Reading. They had been packed off first to Epsom, which they were both to describe to me as a brutal, rough school where there had been a great deal of bullying, then to the Middlesex, which the younger one, Vernon, had entered, in 1897, at the relatively youthful age of eighteen, no doubt he was in a desperate hurry to get away from Epsom. The two brothers had been given no choice as to the profession they were to exercise in life. Each seems to have faced up to the problem in his own way, though it must have been more difficult for Jack, the elder of the two, for he had been expected eventually to take over his father's practice, after first acting as a sort of junior partner under a strict and critical parental eye. A medical career seems often to have been hereditary in those days (Jack would have qualified in about 1900, Vernon five years later, in 1905). Such an arrangement would have avoided the initial expense of having to buy a practice from the outgoing incumbent and then sit about waiting for the first patient to turn up: no doubt a fairly agonising period which might last as long as three to six months for the young doctor who had just put up his

73

plate. Jack would presumably have been able to count on his father's extensive network of patients – he had been in Binfield for the previous thirty years – over as wide an area as was reachable by a gig and a pair of horses, thus avoiding at least the long bleak hours, day by day, waiting, white-coated, in the silence of an empty surgery, among all the polished silver instruments and tools of the trade, in their green and mauve velvet-lined cases, for the sound of the bell marked SURGERY: an experience that had induced the youthful Conan-Doyle to abandon an unassuming street in Southsea after only a year.

Vernon, the younger brother, the youngest member of a family of eight – everything seems to have come to him very young, he met his future wife when he was eighteen, and he qualified when he was only twenty-six – soon after qualifying, seems at least to have made quite a bold bid to escape from the no doubt familiar itineraries of a large Berkshire rural practice. I imagine that, in any case, he had little choice: there would hardly have been room for a second partner in his father's medical establishment. So he had crossed the Channel and had spent from six months to a year 'walking the Paris hospitals'. The phrase, which used to puzzle me as a child – why did he have to *walk* them? Could he not have done some of it just standing up or even sitting down? – was my mother's. My mother, as I have explained elsewhere, was much given to the peculiarities of an inward medical vocabulary as illustrative of belonging to a large hippocratic family: two brothers in practice, one sister married to a naval doctor, another sister, my Aunt Emily, matron of a small hospital in Tunbridge Wells and who had been named, no doubt in anticipation, after a great aunt, Emily Aston, an early pupil, and, in later life, an assiduous correspondent of Florence Nightingale, who had been matron of a hospital in Buenos Aires, where she had died of yellow fever, thus lending the family the lustre of medical sacrifice. The younger Emily did not emulate her aunt, dying in Tunbridge Wells, more prosaically, of cancer, shortly after her retirement.

Such family links no doubt gave my mother the right to refer familiarly, as she constantly did, and with a sort of knowing affection, as if she had long been admitted into all the inner secrets of the place, to the Middlesex, not a county, but a *thing* with the definite article, and to pepper her conversation with letters such as FRCS, quite as mysterious to me, as a child, as 'walking the Paris hospitals'.

Not long after he had returned from Paris, armed with a first-hand intimacy with enlarged and suddenly bursting livers, and with, I suppose, at least a smattering of French, Vernon took up a post in medical administration as Medical Officer of Health in the small town of Clitheroe, a place that, as a result of its damp climate, had a very high rate of tuberculosis (Parisian experience, especially in the *IVme arrondissement* and in *l'Hôtel-Dieu*, would also have prepared him well for that killer disease). It looked like a fairly unpromising start, but I imagine that he had little choice; he had recently married a Greek girl from Corfu whom he had first met when she had been training as a nurse at the Middlesex (both my uncles went through the usual medical procedure of marrying nurses, just as my Aunt Katharine, a nurse, married a doctor, and one too who did not at once have to put up a plate, as he was in the Navy, the plate coming much later, once he was permanently ashore). So he had probably had to take the first job that had presented itself, and a position in public medicine would at least have the advantage of providing him with a regular income – I think even free accommodation went with it – and with avoiding all the expenses involved in purchasing a practice, as well as the uncertainties attendant on first putting up one's plate, however inviting, shining, and well-polished it might be.

Among his administrative duties was that of witnessing each hanging that took place in Lancaster Gaol and of then certifying death. It was not a very exciting job in medical terms, but at least it was one that allowed little margin for error, as a result of a wrong diagnosis or the wrong sort of treatment. He told me, when I was a prep-school boy, that the hanging room was a bit like a gym, and that, like a gym, it smelt of stale sweat, of chalk, and, very faintly, of excrement. Of course, when you think about it, I suppose hanging *is* a sort of gymnastic feat, both on the part of the hangman and of the principal performer: getting the weights just right, springing the trap – my uncle said it made a loud bang, followed by a muffled bump beneath the stage, very like the sound of someone landing on the far side of a wooden horse in a gym. After the bump, he would have to go down below to make sure that everything had gone according to plan. All the time that he had been in Clitheroe, things had gone off all right. He added, for my information – though he had no children of his own, he seemed to have a very keen knowledge of what was likely to be of interest to an inquiring twelve year-old prep-school boy – that the lingering odour of excrement could be attributed to the fact that hanging would cause the main performer to evacuate: a messy business.

My uncle Vernon did not enjoy witnessing hangings, though he told me it was really no worse than preparing for 'the imminent horrors of the football field or some other brutal sport in the boys' changing-room at his House at Epsom. Anyhow, as a twelve-year old schoolboy, I found the changing-room and the hanging-room parallel both interesting and evocative, I am sure it *must* have been just like that. The chalk? Ah yes, the hangman had to put the chalk marks fairly high up on the wall: lavatory tiles painted a dark chocolate brown halfway up, the upper half painted a pale yellow (he would have remembered a thing like that, I much admired his keen eye for minute detail, something that I have always tried to emulate, contributing as it does so much to the credibility of an account of events recalled). The chalk marks, which indicated the height of the person about to drop through the trap, were for the guidance of the hangman. I think my uncle witnessed more than fifty drops. He said it was always a relief to get out into the fresh air afterwards.

Uncle Vernon was no simple, unquestioning patriot like my father. He questioned everything, had a marked aversion for the clergy, and remained lastingly resentful at having been caught up in the RAMC during the First World War. At least he was lucky enough not to have served on the Western Front, spending most of the war in India, where he acquired a very wide knowledge of the various forms of amoebic dysentery, several of which he experienced himself, having caught them from his patients. He had never been strong and his time in India left his health permanently impaired. I have a photograph – I don't know why he had himself photographed, for he hated the army and uniform, I dare-say it was to send to his Greek wife and to his six sisters – of him dating from this unhappy period. He is standing against a background of row upon row of wooden army huts: a stage set background transportable in its entirety from continent to continent, it could as well have been Catterick or Strensall as Rawalpindi or Peshawar. He is a most improbable-looking officer, with his round horn-rimmed glasses, penetrating eyes, the creases of disbelief at the corners of his humorous mouth, and narrow, foxlike (I flatter myself in the belief that I have always looked like him), scholarly face. He is round-shouldered and slovenly, his Sam Browne is much too big for him, and he is uncertain what to do with his swagger stick. He looks a bit like a self-promoted officer in a ramshackle revolutionary army, a Trotsky without a beard and without a hint of military talent.

In the end, I think it must have been some time in the early twenties, once he had got safely back to the longed-for joys of civilian life and domesticity – he was a born civilian, and his advice to me, when I was only eight and had, much to the displeasure of my father, just refused to join the local Cubs, was never to get myself into uniform (something I did my best to achieve, though without success) – my uncle became private physician to a minor public figure, T. P. O'Connor, the Father of the House of Commons and for many years principal Film Censor (every time I saw his sprawling signature, in white letters, against a black background, on the certificate at the beginning of a film, it might be *Ben Hur*, or it might be '*M*', I had a feeling of secret pride; it is true I did not know the great man myself, but my uncle worked with someone famous), an Irish machine politician and keen London socialite, much in demand at fashionable dinner-parties, and for a very long time – forty years, I think – Member for the Scotland Division of Liverpool (though he cannot have spent very much time among his faithful constituents). 'Tay-Pay' was a great traveller, going on lecture tours to North and South America, and my uncle and his medicine bag would go along with him. I think the services of the bag were entirely honorary and rarely called for, 'T.P.' thriving on Irish whiskey. The old man was also President of the Byron Society, an organisation devoted to the promotion of Anglo-Hellenic friendship. Vernon of course had a personal stake in that; some time in the Clitheroe period he had become engaged to and then married Honorine Koskinos, whom the King of Greece – Constantine, I suppose – had personally sent to be trained as a nurse at the Middlesex after her father had been killed in one of the many wars against the Turks: a Turkish scimitar, which had been taken off a dead Turkish officer by her hero father, hung in the hall of my uncle's Chelsea house; it was the first thing that one noticed, its assertive and viciously hooked presence striking a somewhat incongruous and certainly very alarming *entrée* (I used to edge past it as quickly as possible, while keeping it at a prudent distance from which I was able to admire its beautiful jewelled scabbard) to the home of someone as fully committed to the cause of internationalism – he was much involved in the activities of the League of Nations Union and similar bodies – as my uncle Vernon. I suppose the bejewelled scimitar was a sort of domestic monument to Honorine's dead father. The King of Greece had provided a more practical one on behalf of the Koskinos family: as well as paying for Honorine's nursing training, he had extended his generosity to her two young brothers, sending them to Eton as oppidans. The Greek connection had been a very fortunate one for Vernon. As well as bringing him Honorine, it must have put him in the path of T. P. O'Connor in the first place, presumably through the Byron Society. Later, both 'T.P.' and my uncle became regular visitors to Greece, though my aunt did not accompany them on these trips.

Apart from the long-lived journalist and politician – he died in his eighties in 1929, I remember seeing a photograph of him lying in an open coffin and surrounded by hundreds of blazing candles when I was still at the *Beacon* – Vernon seems to have had a prosperous private practice at 43, Glebe Place, Chelsea (the home of the scimitar.) Several of his patients were prominent figures in the London Greek colony: the millionaire George Eumophopoulos, a benefactor of the British Museum, the shipping and trading family of Rallis, and suchlike. They must have rated philhellenism a bit higher than preoccupation with their own health or that of their families, for I don't think Vernon was a very committed doctor, though he was undoubtedly a fashionable one. He had also shown some skill in managing to combine a deliberately restricted private practice with a permanent post in the public sector, for, throughout the Chelsea years and up to the time of his death, he acted as a factory inspector and an industrial doctor concerned with the execution of health and safety regulations, a post, like the early one in Clitheroe, that brought him in a regular income.

Medicine had in the end given Vernon the opportunity to travel all over the place (though he avoided India), as well as providing a convenient entry to the upper reaches of Chelsea society. He liked entertaining and giving elaborate dinner-parties, and he knew a great many artists, fashionable portrait-painters, journalists, critics, and people on the fringes of literary life. 'T.P.' must also have put him in touch with some of the more important figures of the political world, for my sister recalls having met one of the Chamberlains – presumably the fashionable Austen, not the dour Neville, who would hardly have been much at home at one of these no doubt jolly evenings – at one of his dinner-parties. I suppose that, in the twenties and thirties, a doctor with a good address could still cut quite an important figure in London society. He also had close friends among Harley Street consultants who were similarly disposed. He was probably not an outstanding doctor, I don't think he had the right sort of letters after his name – I am sure my mother would have told me if he had had – but he would have known who was and would have been able to tell you whom to go to for this or that (he sent me to someone for the removal of my tonsils when I was nine; when I was fourteen, he had me examined by an eye surgeon, Mr Goulden, the brother of the Tunbridge Wells stationer; and, when I was seventeen and in a bit of a fix, he was at once able to put my mother in touch, at very short notice, with a leading Wimpole Street psychiatrist, Mr Simon). As I have said, Vernon was not much concerned to get new patients; a few wealthy ones, plus the routine factory jobs, would no doubt have been quite enough to enable him to lead a fairly lavish *train de vie*. I was too young ever to have been invited to attend any of his evening functions, but my sister tells me that they were very grand affairs, that Vernon liked dressing up, was very keen on cultivating the social graces, including the art of conversation – Diana had remained tongue-tied the first time she had attended one of these *soirées*, and he had taken her to task afterwards, in a friendly way – and the use of finger bowls, and that he seemed to know about wine and which way round port and madeira had to go, and that sort of thing.

My Aunt Honorine had Greek Afternoons every Thursday from 3 to 6. She was (understandably) a deeply committed royalist and had a signed photograph of King George of the Hellenes prominently displayed on a round table in her drawing-room, doubling up as it were on the jewelled scimitar in the entrance. The King was, I seem to remember, just round the corner – he may even have attended one of the Afternoons. I attended a number of these occasions, which I very much enjoyed, both as an onlooker and an eavesdropper, though totally defeated in the latter capacity. Everyone talked very fast Greek at once, they seemed to be talking Greek *at* one another, and sometimes it sounded as if they were getting very angry, splaying out all five fingers in gestures of contempt, or that is how it looked to me. Of course, these were the first foreigners I had really come across, though there had been an Argentinian boy at one of my prep schools. I had been warned by my uncle never to mention Venizelos in my aunt's presence; I did not know who Venizelos was, but, as my aunt did not like him, I never did. In any case, it would have been hard for me even to have got in a word at one of her Greek Afternoons. These went on right through the war, increasing both in numbers and in the steadily rising volume of noise, as more and more Greek royalists – republicans would not have been admitted to her Thursdays – found there way to London and to 17, Glebe Place. Rationing did not seem to have been a problem, and the machine-gun exchanges – perhaps not quite the right word for a series of competing monologues – were conducted, rather like the prelude to a military operation, a dawn *sortie*, under a thick screen of sweet-smelling Balkan tobacco smoke.

The Afternoons were only brought to an end by my aunt's death, at a fairly advanced age, in the late-1940s. She had outlived Vernon ('Vairnon') by well over a dozen years. Although she had been in England, I think almost continuously from the age of eighteen, her English remained poor and her pronunciation was very erratic; certainly Vernon never had done anything to improve either, finding her strange accent endearing and her mistakes highly amusing. She was a very warm, affectionate and (rather alarmingly) demonstrative person (she was the only member of my family ever to have kissed me, at least as an adult; indeed, she always kissed me at the beginning and the end of each of my visits). I think that she had a soft spot for me, saying that I took after Vernon (I like to think that I did and still do), and, with approval, that I was a good listener. There was not much chance of my *not* being one at any of her Greek Afternoons.

When she died, she left me quite a lot of money, tied up in the form of an annuity it is still coming in, twice yearly, as if the ebullient, tubby little Greek lady, with her sharp black eyes and sallow complexion, had managed as it were to prolong herself a further forty years beyond her death, revisiting me and reminding me, at two fixed points of the year, of those cacophonous Thursdays, right into my own seventies: the sums involved are trifling, about £40 a time ('Mrs Swindale's Estate'), but the bi-annual recall both of my prudent Aunt Honorine and of my own past fecklessness, is a bit like the expected visit, at a given date, as the seasons come round, of some very old friend. If the cheques stopped, it would be rather as if she had died a second time, even under the unfamiliar disguise, both impersonal and chillingly legal, of 'Mrs Swindale' (the first time I saw that, I wondered to whom it was referring.) She had gone to considerable pains to come by a financial arrangement which would, as she saw it, work out the best to my long-term advantage. She was naturally cautious as far as money was concerned, as well as shrewd, and an incident – to me, a very small one, hardly even worth calling it that, but not to her – that had occurred when I had been coming up to twenty-two had been for her both a revelation and a warning of what the future might hold in store.

It happened on New Year's Day, 1939. It was a miserable, wet, blustery Sunday morning, with a low grey sky and that particular hopelessness that one associates with an English Sunday in winter. I can still recall the beddraggled *Sunday Pictorial* poster: WAR THIS YEAR? (at this precise moment a military ambulance, painted brown, with a huge red cross on both its sides and on its roof, scurried down the empty, wind-swept road, with a sense of extreme urgency, as if to provide an answer) in large red letters on what had been a white background, flapping in the mud among the swirling empty cigarette packets under Charing Cross Bridge. I had been walking along the Embankment in the direction of Chelsea with my Merton friend, Leonard Coddington. Len and I both had appalling hang-overs; we had been up till one in the morning, drinking in a pub full of tall guardsmen, their young, pink noses protruding from just below the level of the polished peaks of their caps, their eyes invisible, and of old ladies in ratskin black hats who, at the stroke of midnight, had cried noisy New Year's tears into their large gins. Len, in fact, had stayed up all night, heading for Covent Garden. I had called off at two to get a few hours' sleep in a Torrington Square boarding house. 1939 had seemed quite promising in the festive warmth of the crowded pub; but now, a few hours on, under the lowering sky, it had *aged*, had lost its innocence, and seemed to offer nothing but a sort of dull foreboding. Although we did not speak, walking in silence, in both our minds there could have been little doubt as to the answer to the question in large blood-red letters. Still, it was better not to have put our thoughts into words, it would only have made matters worse. But, as if to confirm them, as we turned off the Embankment into a side street, we saw coming towards us a shabby, dejected, hunched up young man in a long dirty mac, with a dead, desperate face the colour of wax, pushing an old pram in which there appeared to be a baby, well wrapped-up against the foul morning. His expressionless eyes looked right through us, as though he too had actually seen ahead of him, and lurking behind us, dogging our footsteps, what was coming. I suppose there might have been some tiny hope for the future inside the pram, but it certainly looked as if the young man was not all that keen on *that* sort of future. Paternity seemed to fill him with a dumb despair.

We were both desperate for a drink and the previous evening had cleared us out. Len knew no one in London. There seemed to be only one way out: call on my Greek aunt and ask to borrow ten shillings. Luckily, when we got to Glebe Place, we found her in; it was already quite late in the morning and she had just got back from the Greek Cathedral; she had not taken off her black velvet hat and her black gloves. She kissed me on both cheeks and wished me a Happy New Year (I don't think she got the formula quite right, 'prosperous' as I recollect, rather than 'happy'; still it was well meant.) She was dressed in her best Sunday black silk. I introduced Len as a friend from College; she seemed to have difficulty coming to terms with this piece of information, subjecting him to a critical, sharp, black-eyed appraisal, starting at the feet and ending up at his sodden, uncombed hair that was hanging in a few long wet wisps. He was not looking his best: both his tie and his mac had gone in the course of the previous evening or the early hours of the morning; there was a large tear, with the lining exposed, in the left elbow of his jacket, which had the middle button missing and was covered in mud at the sleeve; he had a cut lip which had bled onto the frayed collar of his shirt. My aunt hesitated, ever so slightly, before offering him a chair and a glass of very dry sherry. Len did not like sherry, he thought it was a class drink (Len's father ran a corner-shop in Leicester and lived with his mistress, he was a widower. In the vacations, Len stayed in their house, paying them a rent of 35/- a week: I remember pointing out that he could get digs in London for about that, but he was still very suspicious of London, or of anywhere apart from Leicester). His hand was shaking, and some of the sherry spilled onto the arm of the chair. I could see that he was very ill at ease, he was not used to foreigners and showed no sign of wanting to become so, and he had just spotted the silver-framed photograph of the exiled King of the Hellenes and the sprawling signature, in very blue ink, across the tight chest of the uniform, the medals, the crosses and the sashes. He had missed the scimitar, but the photograph in its silver frame was a *double* provocation. My college friend was very left-wing and had joined the Left Book Club. My aunt rather pointedly asked me about my parents, my sister, my cousins, drawing out the roll-call in order to exclude Len. Then we talked a bit about the foul weather, and finally I plucked up the courage to ask if she could lend me ten shillings, as we were in a bit of a fix. She made no difficulty, getting out her best black bag and handing me over the little sepia note, the progress of which from her bag to my inner pocket was closely watched by Len, who had at last taken his eyes off the royal countenance. After a decent interval, in the course of which she asked my friend if he too had done history, she kissed me on both cheeks, and we took our leave.

As soon as we were outside, Len commented accusingly, as if it had been *my* fault, anyhow guilt by association, that this had been the first time – and he hoped it would be the last – that he had been inside a Fascist house. I didn't argue, letting him have his say. He soon cheered up and we went off to a pub which was very near the river. 1939 did not look quite so bleak after all; from the desolate gloom of the morning, it had suddenly jerked back to its lusty new-born howl of just after midnight; indeed, it stayed on a jerky course, like a barometer, swinging wildly from hope to despair, for much of the year, till that dreadful day in late-August. I felt grateful to my aunt, I had never done anything like this before, it had been very much a shot in the dark, and it had come off. But, once in the warmth of the pub – I did not give her much thought. What I did not then know – but I would know it soon enough, it went like a bush fire through the length and breadth of my mother's family: my mother, one uncle, five aunts, ten cousins – was that I had left her giving her favourite nephew a great deal of thought. She had concluded from the incident – and she was perfectly right – that I had no sense of money, and so the annuity had been set up to protect me from myself. Like a gallant little watchdog, it has gone on steadfastly doing that for nearly forty years.

I visited the house in Glebe Place soon after my aunt's death, accompanied by the executor, my chartered accountant cousin, who had the keys. We had come to collect a silver object, a small, inlaid Greek snuff-box that I had always liked handling – I forgot to mention that Honorine regularly took snuff – sneezing vigorously between fast-delivered sentences at the Greek Afternoons, some of the very dark brown snuff falling down the front of her embroidered white blouse – and that she had left me in her will. The scimitar in its jewelled scabbard, the photograph of the exiled King, and the dark-faced ikon in the far corner were still in place.

Apart from the house in Chelsea, my uncle and aunt acquired, not long before Vernon's sudden death in his sleep in 1936, one year after that of my father, at the early age of fifty-five, a pretty weekend cottage at Etchingham in Sussex. They crammed it with handsome antiques which, in the semi-darkness (the cottage had tiny windows) one tended to stumble into – they both had a very good eye for bargains. There was a large garden at the back and they took on a full-time gardener to look after it (I could not have pictured either of them, especially the utterly urban Honorine, with secateurs, gardening gloves and a shallow wooden basket for weeds). Vernon's near neighbour was Rudyard Kipling, whom he *loathed* (this further endeared my uncle to me, the author of 'If' was common ground for detestation), and with his scathing remarks about his celebrated neighbour and the demi-battleship that he had had put up in his garden, he seemed to be furthering, rather by hints and nudges than in so many words, that sense of complicity that seemed to bind us together in a secret society of two, something that was very much an uncle's privilege, especially in the case of one who had no children of his own. It was almost as if he had been saying: 'We both know that we are in this thing together, but we must not tell anyone about it, not even your mother', which was very clever of him, for what he *really* meant, and I knew he meant, was not my mother, but my father.

When I was fourteen, I was the privileged and, indeed, delighted, spectator to a scene, quite unrehearsed, and all the better for that, that took place early on a Monday morning on Etchingham Station. I was going back to London with my uncle, my aunt was staying on in the country during the week. There was a long queue at the ticket-office; an oldish man with a drooping white moustache and very shaggy black eyebrows, wearing a long black overcoat with a velvet collar, and carrying a silver-topped stick, came in in a hurry, pushing straight to the head of the queue, without so much as an apology, and asking, in a loud, confident voice, for a First Class Single to London. The man at the ticket office requested him, quite politely, to take his place right at the end of the queue and wait his turn, there was no need to rush, the train was not due in for a quarter of an hour. 'Do you realise who I am?' stormed the old man, holding his ground at the front. This proved too much for the patience of the ticket clerk (who, no doubt, had had to put up with this sort of behaviour on any number of previous occasions). 'I know who you are, Mr Rudyard Bloody Kipling', he shouted, '*and* you can bloody well take your place in the queue like everybody else'. No public scene could have been more perfectly set up for my Uncle Vernon, who promptly took over, loudly congratulating the man behind the window: 'Well said! Well said!', to the visible consternation of the shocked Monday morning City commuters. There was even better to come: the great man decided not to travel that day after all, and flounced out of the station, purple with rage. He had already sent his chauffeur back with his car, so I suppose he had to walk all the way back to the house with the demi-battleship in the garden, England's National Shrine. I could see from the glint in his grey eyes, behind his innocent-looking spectacles, that my uncle had enormously enjoyed the occasion, that he had been glad of such an unexpectedly large audience, including that of his appreciative nephew, in this small country station, and that the whole episode, suitably embellished, would soon be part of his after-dinner repertoire over port and madeira. Well, it was a good story, and it was something thus to have laid an impious hand on one of our more sacred National Monuments. How shocked my father would have been over the station scene! But, of course, I never told him about it. I told my mother, who smiled indulgently: 'Vernon has never grown up'. The unspoken complicity between Vernon and myself made me feel like an adult, and this was very flattering. Indeed, when I was still at my prep school, he would *treat* me like an adult, coming out with such remarks as: 'A lot of people will tell you that their schooldays were the happiest time of their lives, always to be looked back to. That is absolute rot, you'll never be so unhappy again, the thing is to get them over as early as possible'. He had certainly acted on this sound advice. He would advise me to go out of my way to avoid boxing and the sweaty horrors of the gym ('I'll write you out a medical certificate, but, Sh, don't tell your parents'); and he suggested ways of getting my temperature up in order to get out of cricket or football (there is much to be said for having a medical uncle and I was lucky enough to have *two*, both of them very ready with professional tips of this useful kind: Vernon did indeed get me out of boxing and the gym. His brother, Jack, helped, as I have pointed out, to keep me out of the Services in 1939).

When, shortly after the Kipling scene, I was about to start at Shrewsbury, we (that is, my mother, my sister and I: 'Frank is so sorry he could not come, he would love to have seen the cottage') went over to Etchingham for Sunday lunch; and, just as we were getting ready to leave, after tea, my uncle beckoned to me to come over to an even darker corner at the far end of the room. As I have said, he liked playing the conspirator in partnership with me. I think that also he saw in me a fellow rebel, one to kick against the pricks of collective conformisms; and, indeed, right up to now, I suppose I have always seen myself as his pupil in this important respect. After fumbling about in the trouser-pocket of his three-piece grey flannel suit (which went with his eternal grey trilby) he fished out the then princely sum of five shillings: 'Take this', he said, in his agreeable voice, the voice of irreverence and doubt, 'you'll need it, I expect you'll HATE the place, I certainly HATED the one they sent me to (I always liked the way he managed to associate me with his THEYs). As far as Shrewsbury was concerned, he was only partly right in his prediction: I hated my House, but quite liked the school, even more the town on the other side of it and the wonderful freedom of running over the red mud of the Shropshire countryside. Vernon would have approved of cross-country running, you did it for *yourself*.

I can remember little about Vernon and Honorine during my time at Shrewsbury, save that I stayed with them during the crisis provoked by the threatened libel suit, when I had had to go and see Mr Simon and his colleague. It was yet another case of Uncle Vernon to the rescue. As I have said, he knew all the right people; I think he would even have known how to get me off from being hanged. My mother had implicit faith in him when faced with any sort of crisis, medical or otherwise: 'I'll get in touch with Vernon'. I think he must have died – it was very sudden and quite unexpected – during the Oxford term, some time in 1936, for I cannot recall going to the funeral (I had not been to that of my father, the previous year, my mother had not told me about it till a fortnight after it had taken place; she was very sensible about funerals, saying there was no point in making a great thing of them, it would be of no help to the principal participant, and if you made a fuss over them, that would only induce a lot of noise and a disagreeable lack of restraint: my mother hated any sort of excess). I was just nineteen when my uncle died: still a bit too young to have been admitted, *de plein pied*, to his circle of dining friends. I don't know what he would have made of me at that age, had I been accorded full *droits de table*. Certainly, my table manners were not up to much: I was a messy eater, spilling a lot, and I was still terribly shy and *gauche*. I would have been quite tongue-tied in conversation, and I would have drunk too much wine, gulping it down, without even bothering to look at the year, which would not have meant anything to me in any case. I wish he had lived just a little bit longer, so that I could have told him about *my* years in the army and how I had managed to get by, and about my experiences, not of 'walking the Paris hospitals', but of walking Paris itself, from end to end, from Boulogne-Billancourt to Vincennes, from Montrouge to Saint-Ouen. I loved his sense of mischief, his alert irreverence, his habit of questioning everything, his ever-inquiring cosmopolitanism. He was a very good uncle to me. I hope I have turned out a good pupil.

Jack and Frances

Like his younger brother, my red-haired, peppery Uncle Jack always treated me as a fellow-conspirator, from the time I was eleven or twelve, and, in this case, our shared complicity was much longer-lasting than that with Vernon, for Jack lived to the age of eighty, dying, still in harness, some time in the second half of the 1950s. His wife, Aunt Frances, would have dearly liked to have been included, in her own right, in an association that had managed to survive my years as a schoolboy and an undergraduate, but I was never prepared to admit her into any role that involved myself. Jack and I got on best when the two of us were together, either on his rounds, visiting private patients or emergency cases, or, later, once I was at Oxford, when we went to the pub. There was a tacit understanding between the two of us that there were a certain number of things that were best kept from my aunt: these would include some of his immediate comments on his wealthier female patients, the sheen and the degree of cleanliness of their underwear, the undulations of their intimacies, what they *thought* was wrong with them, what *he* thought was wrong with them, and his magnificently detailed descriptions of the domestic arrangements of some of his *less* affluent ones: the washing facilities, or the lack of them, the ornaments on the mantelpiece, the pictures on the walls, the sea-shells on the window-ledges, the framed texts, the Coronation biscuit tins, in fact a pretty complete inventory of the appearance and the contents of the bedroom in a primitive rural cottage, or in a recently built council house.

My uncle's practice in Theale was a very varied one, stretching across a very wide social spectrum, taking in Church and Chapel, the retired wealthy, the rural poor, tradesmen and shopkeepers and workers in light industries. He used to tell me this was why he liked being a doctor, he got little enjoyment out of diagnosis, which, he

Richard Cobb, blackberrying near Tunbridge Wells, September 1939.

By the Hill & St. Leonards Church, Colchester.

The Revd Henry Carter (left) *and the Revd Gilbert Newcomen* (right) *with the Superintendant of St Leonard's Sunday School.*

St Leonard's House, (on the left), *Hythe Hill, Colchester.*

Frank Papé.

Francis and Dora Cobb, his parents, at Brighton.

Primus Cobb on Clacton Pier.

Charles and Catharine Cobb, Richard Cobb's grandparents.

Richard Cobb his sister Diana with Jenny and Mills, the groom.

Uncle Vernon Swindale.

Uncle Jack Swindale.

claimed, was in most cases self-evident; but he liked getting into other peoples' houses and picking up all sorts of odd items of gossip. He was an excellent observer of interiors, and his ears were well attuned to the variations of accents and of local popular speech. He seemed to feel particularly at home with the local Berkshire whine, a cross between cockney and the wheezing, asthmatic sounds coming from the nearby West Country. Of course he had spent much of his career in Berkshire; but, later, I found his ear equally well attuned to the accents of East Kent, of South Hampshire, and, late in life, to the querulous tones of Horsepath and Headington. He was also very strong, very observant, on the minutiae of class: he told me he never had *Punch* in the waiting-room of his surgery, his poorer patients would not have liked it, it was a middle-class paper with jokes about people who dropped their H's. But the *Field* did not cause class antagonism, and the *Horse and Hound* was pretty well inter-class. *Revielle* was always a good stand-by, *Picture Post* he thought, was pretty safe. He went to the big, early Gothic revival Anglican church on Sundays, to be *seen*, because his more prosperous patients attended Matins there, but he maintained friendly relations with the Chapel people through the local chemist, who was a Baptist.

Medical gossip and social observation of this kind was for my privileged ears alone, it was part of an association that he assumed I would accept, from the age of twelve onwards. Of course I felt enormously flattered in being the recipient of these off-the-cuff observations, in between two or three afternoon and early-evening calls to patients scattered all over the pretty, undulating, well-wooded South Berkshire countryside. Jack was as talkative as he was observant, and he always had the most to say once he had climbed back into the driving seat of his car after twenty minutes or half an hour with a patient. I did not find the wait in the car at all boring; I would get my reward hot press from some overheated and evil-smelling interior, or from some well-appointed boudoir carrying wafts of Chanel or eau-de-cologne, once I spotted the familiar figure, in the grey trilby hat pulled well over his forehead and sitting straight on his head, grey suit, and little old-fashioned medical bag — it must have come from his father — with its gold clasps, coming down the steps, or down an impressive drive, after the front-door, showing a brief ray of yellow light, had quietly closed behind him. If there was an extra twinkle in his very blue, slightly globulous and protruding eyes, I would know that there would be something especially good about to come.

Following him on his rural, urban, and suburban rounds was a bit like being a GP at one remove, without the tedium, the fatigue, all the familiar rigmarole with stethoscope and thermometer or blood pressure, or looking at tongues, or making people say *Ninety-nine*. Jack always drove rather slowly, as if to give the latest story time to develop in its full luxuriance before he disappeared behind the next stained-glass-pannelled front-door or stately white frontage. I don't think he would have driven any faster had he been alone; but, certainly, in the company of his nephew, he never seemed at all pressed to get back home. In between anecdotes of bedrooms and sick-beds, enormous quilts and piled-up pillows, over-flowing chamber-pots, and simmering kettles, he would point out buildings of interest, churches (including one that, he said, had a very realistic looking fly on its East window), follies, ducal gateways and heraldic entrances, and houses, magnificent, modest, unkempt, peeling, ugly, jerry-built, where he had other patients. He was a good judge both of architecture and period and could have taken me through the length and breadth of South Berkshire mapping out the ribbon development of the 1930s and the solid achievements of the Edwardians. On one of my visits, when I was fourteen, he took a day off and drove me over to Oxford, showing me all the colleges; I was so impressed by what I saw that I decided there and then that I would like to go up there, rather than to Cambridge, where my Aunt Mabel had been. He was pleased, because he did not like – indeed, detested – Mabel.

I have seldom enjoyed anyone's company so much, whether at twelve, fourteen, or in my twenties. Of course, he was well aware of the fact, there was a natural community between us; he was an inquisitive man, and recognised in me a fellow-sufferer. He also had a deliciously irreverent and equally communicable sense of humour. Although he was said at times to be very bad-tempered – and his eyes *did* bulge in a rather alarming way – I at least never saw him angry. When I was twelve, after having had a row with my father, on the subject of religion – something that he did not take lightly – I decided to run away to Theale, taking the train from Tonbridge to Reading, and ringing up my uncle from the station. He came to fetch me, as if he had been expecting me, and no more was said. He got in touch with his sister that evening. I stayed a fortnight. I suppose it is a good bit easier to be an uncle than to be a father. Anyhow, I felt completely at home with him. He seemed to be amused by my flight, adding that it showed I had a sense of initiative.

I have no idea whether he was a good doctor, he was certainly not a specialist, and I don't think he followed the medical journals (he took the *Lancet*, mainly to impress his patients, it was displayed in the waiting-room to the surgery), but he must have picked up a lot of elementary wisdom at diagnosis in the course of an unusually long career as a GP – he was still in practice in his late-seventies, with half-a-dozen patients as old as himself, I think they must have been reassured by his long years in the profession and there may well be something in it, an elderly doctor has been up against the full range of the commoner maladies – in very varied areas and among a very wide social range of patients. He used to tell me that a doctor was one of the few people who, in the course of a single day, could cross every gradation of class. He was certainly no apostle of cheap medicine, pocketing his fee with a dismissive gesture, but I think he gave more time and more attention to his poorer patients than to his affluent ones, both because he thought there was likely to be much more the matter with them and because he preferred their company, and found them more interesting. Later, as an undergraduate, I was impressed by the warmth with which 'Dr Swindale', or just 'the Doctor' would be greeted in the Lounge Bars of two or three ugly mock-tudor pubs set in the grey anonymity of the council estates and the jerry-built terraced houses of Waterlooville, on the chalky heights above Portsmouth and Southsea. There cannot have been many well-to-do patients in such a locality.

Of course, there were occasions when he did not quite hit it off with the locals. I can well remember one such, some time in 1937, when I had come over from Oxford to stay with him for a long weekend. We had gone to one of the nearby pubs (I seem to remember that the landlord was an ex-Naval CPO), where the wireless was full on in all the bars, relaying the Coronation Service of George VI. We thought of going elsewhere, but concluded that there would probably be no escape from the noise that made all attempts at conversation impossible. At the point when the new King was taking the oath to uphold this or that: the Church Established, the Act of Succession, or whatever – stumbling over the words and struggling desperately with his stutter, Jack and I could not restrain our hilarity, it would not have happened if I had not caught his eye and had not seen him stuffing a handkerchief into his mouth. 'The Doctor' and his nephew had got the popular mood badly wrong and we had had to make for the door in a hurry: the looks that accompanied our backs as we beat a hasty retreat from the bar reminded me of those of the commuters on Etchingham Station on the occasion of the Kipling incident. We kept clear of that pub for the rest of my stay but, I think Jack went back there eventually. I imagine that our disrespect for the new monarch was soon forgotten. Crossing the frontiers of class can be a dangerous business, even for doctors, and overt irreverence can lead to trouble; both my uncles were rather dangerous companions in this respect.

I know little about the basic economics of General Practice in the last three or four decades of private medicine and of the family doctor, but my uncle's frequent moves from place to place would seem to have been in defiance of the more obvious priorities of a medical career. It might be presumed that to build up a good practice was a matter of time and patience and that the longer one stayed in a single locality, the more patients one would acquire, even extending from parents to children, and thence to grandchildren. I have referred elsewhere to the medical dynasties of Tunbridge Wells. This does not seem to have been Jack's approach to success as a GP. He seemed to have been frequently on the move, as if he had actually enjoyed the novelty, surely a bit frayed with the passage of years, of putting up his plate in a new place. I don't know how many year's he had remained in his father's practice in Binfield. When I first got to know him, he seemed to have been well established in Theale, and had been doing well enough to have taken on a very big house on the main street, almost opposite the extraordinary church, and a young partner just out of medical school. Having started in Berkshire, he may have been eager to get back there. Certainly it was the only time, at least to my knowledge, that he ever had a partner. For the rest of his professional career, he would be a lone flier. In between times, in the twenties, he had had surgeries first in Margate, then in Ramsgate. Something had gone wrong in the course of this double seaside interlude, my mother referring darkly to some scandal that was not fit for childrens' ears. It may have been something to do with a female patient (later, in Theale, he told me that he always kept the door of his consulting-room wide open if he were examining a woman ('You can't be too careful', and that, as an additional precaution, he would make sure of the presence, within sight, of a County nurse) or it could have been related to Income Tax returns which had not been quite straightfor-ward. Anyhow, there had been something unethical that had reached the ears of my mother and her sisters, two of whom, Emily and Mabel, had eagerly retailed the news to a wider family audience, commenting that it had not come as much of a surprise, they had always expected something of the sort. There were obscure currents of enmity, going back many years, perhaps even to childhood, between Jack, Emily and Mabel (There was only a year between Jack and the latter, Jack having been born in 1874, Mabel in 1875, so that rivalry between the two of them could have developed perhaps from such close childhood proximity). My mother was more indulgent: I remember the words 'Poor Jack' coming up pretty often over lunch, my father refraining from comment, but looking pained (so, of course, it could not have been 'poor Jack's' fault, but just some sort of professional carelessness, such as a wrong prescription: my mother had a soft spot for both her brothers and often referred to the red-haired one as 'a bit of a scamp'). I never found out what had happened. I am pretty sure Vernon had been 'called in'; that would have been the term used. Anyhow, Jack had left the bracing twin East Kent resorts rather hurriedly. Theale had followed, then, after that, Waterlooville, a choice that was regarded within the closely-observed family circle, as in some way bad form medically, as if he had been poaching on Uncle Percy's practice down in Southsea, though the two localities seemed pretty far apart, both in mileage and in clientèle. Jack could not be said to have set himself up on his brother-in-law's immaculate doorstep (whitened first thing every morning, no doubt a naval habit), though I have heard the expression used; and most of Percy's patients were retired officers from the navy, their wives and their families: the white doorstep must have signalled to those who could read such things that Surgeon-Commander Alderson RN (Retd) was in residence and available. The naval connection certainly did not extend inland to Waterlooville (save perhaps for the ex-CPO landlord).

There may have been further moves. At this point I temporarily lose track of my uncle, who seems to have been something of a medical carpet-bagger, carrying his plate in his ancient Gladstone outfit. Maybe he enjoyed the challenge of the unknown, the excitement of starting afresh; or perhaps he just liked travelling through the South-East and the Home Counties, varying the menu as he went along: a rural practice, a suburban one, the undoubted promise offered by a seaside place, with many retired residents and a cluster of prep schools (I am surprised that he never had a go at Seaford or Eastbourne; I suppose they were already over-subscribed), the neutral zone of Waterlooville or Theale. There is a gap of perhaps as much as twenty years before Jack finally came to rest in Windmill Road, Headington, a totally uninspiring street running down from the traffic-lights at the cross-roads in the direction of four hospitals placed strategically at the bottom. Jack had a surgery – it must have been cut out of the pantry – in a tiny, rather mean little semi-detached house three quarters of the way down and fairly close to the hospitals. It may have been their proximity which had dictated this final choice. By then my uncle had lost all his red hair, which had been replaced, on the top of his large head, by little white porcine bristles, making him look a good deal more presentable outside than in his home. A strange effect of his baldness was to accentuate his Swindale appearance and to make him look much more like my mother. It was in this wretched little house that he died, alone (the milkman raised the alarm after a couple of days), at the age of eighty.

Unlike his brother Vernon, Jack was not at all house-proud. He seemed to camp in a succession of houses rather than live in them. So observant of other peoples' interiors, he seems to have been quite indifferent to his own; indeed, as far as I could make out, almost *any* excuse to spend as little time *in* it as possible seems to have been eagerly welcomed by him. I am sure this was the reason why he clung on so desperately to a handful of patients right up to the end (he cannot have needed them in order to make two ends meet, I think he left quite a lot of money): they would have provided him a pretext to get out of the little house, even at a time when he found it more and more difficult to negotiate the steep rise up towards the traffic-lights. The last time I saw the two of them together – and my aunt was already very ill – he said that he had a couple of patients to look up, both of them bedridden (it looked very much as if Aunt Frances would soon be in a similar condition), and suggested that I might like to walk up the hill with him. Once we were out on the road, something of the old twinkle appeared in his faded blue eyes, beneath the brim of the grey trilby: 'Let's go to one of the pubs on the main road', which is what we did.

I think the likeliest explanation of all these apparently incoherent moves – rather like those of a clockwork mouse that had been overwound, as it shoots off, first in one direction, then in another, turning in on itself half-way through, – may lie elsewhere, not with Jack, but with his wife. My Aunt Frances was not an easy person and she seems to have been well-endowed all her life with a capacity to fall out with *all* her neighbours, *all* the local tradesmen, indeed with pretty well everyone who mattered, each new departure bringing a sense of relief to the inhabitants of the most recent place to have been vacated. She seems to have left a trail of wreckage behind her wherever she went, so that there could be no going back, it always had to be on and further on. After travelling all those tens of thousands of miles from New Zealand to England, her displacements, with her husband and her son, became more modest: thirty miles, eighty miles, twenty miles. I cannot help thinking that *she* had been behind the move to Waterlooville, in the knowledge that it would have upset my Aunt Katharine and her husband, the naval doctor down in Southsea. Frances was also a constant, but pretty ineffective, trouble-maker within the circle of my mother's family. My sister and I were assigned a minor role, we could be trotted out, on the right occasion, as points of comparison with the other Swindale children, our cousins. She would enthuse, by letter (in green ink), on any academic successes that had come my way, and my sister's triumphs at tennis would be exploited in an effort to underline the inferior showing of her other nieces. The music would be attuned to the ear of the recipient; the nieces and nephews were themselves only pawns in her campaign, which was directed primarily at my Aunt Mabel, through her children. It must have annoyed her that she got so little response.

Within my mother's family, her efforts were more a matter of mirth than of indignation, and Aunt Frances became a well-established figure of fun, her triple-pronged campaigns of mischief-making relayed, with amusement, from one intended victim to the other, and then to the next in line of fire ('Susan, did you know what Auntie Frances said about you in her last letter to me? I'll read it out to you'). It never seemed to have occurred to her that the recipients of the letters in green ink (and very poor spelling) might actually compare notes. By the time I was ten or eleven, her position within the family as a slightly comical figure had been further secured, indeed, enthroned, as a result of the truly frightful presents which she was in the regular habit of inflicting on her nieces and nephews: second-hand objects, often clothing, marked with sinister-looking stains, rusty tricycles, clockwork toys with their springs broken, girls' prams with a wheel missing, dolls that were in the process of losing their stuffing, hideous cracked vases, cushions that had seen better days and that had been much sat upon so that they gave only thin comfort, things that must have been obtained, after long prospection, from the parish jumble-sales and flea-markets of Portsmouth and Southsea (she would have diligently scoured both), Waterlooville, Theale, and Reading, making of Christmas and birthdays (she never missed these) seasons and days both of fear and enquiring expectation: what *new* horror would be revealed once the festive paper and the red ribbons had been unwrapped and undone? (The care that had gone into the wrapping somehow added to the shock that followed, one could almost picture her, seated in her blue armchair and dressed in a pale green blouse, preparing the package with the same grim humour as a crank or a terrorist might devise a letter-bomb or set the fuse of an explosive parcel). She never lowered her exigent standards in the predictable awfulness of her choice.

What was the *matter* with Aunt Frances? What had originally fuelled her constantly renewed stocks of resentment? Why did she try so hard at what could only be a losing game? Why did she have it in so for most of her husband's family? And were the dreadful presents meant to convey a clear message of insult and contempt?

I can only hazard a few suggestions. I think the rancour must have set in very early on, at the time of her marriage, or very shortly after it, following the realization that, despite her efforts (probably clumsy and gauche) she was simply not going to be accepted by Jack's married sisters who – my mother included – were fairly arrant snobs. Frances, from an uncertain background somewhere near Nelson, in South Island, would simply not have passed muster. The general view among that fierce tribunal would have been that the impulsive Jack had once more made a fool of himself, letting the Swindale side down in the process, as he had been prone to do ever since adolescence, by allowing himself to be caught by some scheming Antipodean nurse (hardly an adventuress, surely?) who did not come from the top drawer and spoke with a twanging accent (later, the suggestion that she molly-coddled her only child, my cousin Roland, would be added to the indictment). It was a collective judgment that was rather cruel and certainly uncharitable. Looking back over a great many years, I find my aunt rather pathetic and silly. I suppose that, once in this country, and married to Jack, she had made overtures to her husband's relatives, and that these had been (politely, I am sure, but coldly) rejected. She had tried her best, and it had been no use. Initially, at least, she must have had a fairly justifiable sense of grievance; the trouble was that she would not disarm. Poor Auntie Frances! She wasn't given much of a chance. Still, I could sympathize with my Uncle Jack, an intelligent man who was also a very good observer; and I could appreciate why he liked getting *out* so much. He was also quite as much of a snob as his rival from earliest days, his sister Mabel. Of course, when we were together, we never talked about his wife: it was a subject that we avoided out of some common intuition. And, in any case, Frances would make quite a fuss of me when I was staying there, even to the extent of offering to cook me all the things I liked best – this was the worst of it, for I had then to be seen eating them. I could even see vaguely just why Jack hated Mabel so much. She had married well.

The relationship between an uncle and a nephew is generally an easy, relaxed one, if only because it is intermittent, can be interrupted at short notice, and because there are at all times readily-available exits. An uncle may be ambitious for a nephew, may indeed rejoice in his successes, while encouraging him to pursue this or that line; but he does not have to worry about his future career. I was certainly very fortunate in my two Swindale uncles, and they were both very good to me and for me, treating me like an adult long before I was one or behaved like one. I could talk to them about anything, and there was an altogether happy companionship in our relations. Jack never attempted to persuade me of the advantages of a medical career, for which, as he had observed early on, my extraordinary clumsiness, my inability to deal with the simplest objects, made me entirely unsuited.

But Jack, who was so easy-going with me, even encouraging in me my natural irreverence, was an extremely severe and demanding father to his son, Roland, like my sister, seven years my senior (so that, by the time I had turned up at Theale, the most severe storms had blown themselves out). My uncle, who had been a reluctant doctor and had had medicine imposed upon him by his father, decided, I think almost from Roland's birth, that his son should follow him in the profession. With that in mind, Roland was sent off to Bradfield, where he failed pretty well every exam and which he left with a pitiable academic record. However, his father would not give in: Roland was to be a doctor. Roland did not *want* to be a doctor; the only attraction, in his eyes, of a career as a GP, was an excuse to spend a lot of working time driving a car. But why could he not drive a car *without* being a doctor? It was no use, his father was adamant, and, at eighteen, poor Roland was packed off to Cambridge, to work under a crammer, in order to obtain entrance to the University and to a College. I think Roland spent something like two years in this dim academic borderland, not *of* the University, but *near* it, making friends with young Magdalene bloods who drove fast cars, and playing a great deal of golf and leading a very active social life: his father gave him a good allowance. After Roland had failed the Little Go, or whatever it was called, five or six times, his father was at last induced to throw up the sponge. All right, Roland would *not* be a doctor. My cousin, charming, generous, very good-looking, but not very bright, was very good with cars, putting them together and taking them to pieces, and his ambition was to work in a garage. His father would not hear of it, he was not going to have a son a *mechanic*. He did, however, indulge Roland to the extent of buying him a new red sports car, a splendid-looking vehicle, what the French used to call *un torpédo*, with polished golden pipes curling out of its sides, and in which, unannounced, on a summer afternoon, he visited my prep school in Crowborough, accompanied by my sister, who, like the driver, was wearing goggles: a spectacular visit that very much enhanced my prestige with the other boys.

Anyhow, Roland was not allowed to work in a garage. I think for some time he had had to hang about at home, keeping out of his father's way – Jack seems to have been more attached than ever to his afternoon and early-evening calls during this difficult period –and being rather indulged by his mother, and relieving his boredom by long spells on the golf course. In the end a compromise was reached. His father bought him a sheep-farm near Hawke's Bay, in North Island. I think his mother's family must have been involved in the decision, which turned out to have been a very happy one. Roland liked sheep-farming, I think he even liked sheep, and he married a New Zealand girl: I remember a photograph of him, in a grey top hat, standing on an open wooden balcony, and looking very happy, and a bit like the Prince of Wales: he had the same engaging grin. He came back to Europe at the beginning of the war, having volunteered for the New Zealand Division and being given a commission in REME; I believe he had quite a happy war, lying underneath lorries and scout-cars and helping to repair tanks. Once demobilized he spent some years farming in Devon. He came up from there for the wedding of one of my sister's children, making audible irreverent remarks throughout the service, which was taken by another of my sister's children, who was a parson (he ribbed her about that at the reception). He was quite as irreverent as his father. Eventually, he went back to New Zealand – I think he is still there – living all by himself, near a lake, with his own boat, and doing a great deal of fishing. He never acquired a New Zealand accent, despite all the years spent there. His daughters became Catholics, a fact that he managed to conceal from his father, who would have been horrified.

FIVE

Percy House

I LIKED to feel that no one knew about my recently discovered secret retreat. Of course, some people did, my mother and my sister at least; but it still offered me the comforting security of what – in more dramatic times and in a more dangerous country – might have been described as a 'safe house'. Certainly this slight sense of mystery with which I liked to surround the place added to its attraction as far as I was concerned. As I walked, with what I imagined to be an urgent, indeed, visible, sense of purpose, as if I had been engaged on some important, but very private, mission, I flattered myself that no casual onlooker would have been able to guess for what undertaking I was stepping out so vigorously on a steady uphill climb. Of course, there was in fact absolutely no reason why anyone should have taken any notice of me – and no one ever did – it wasn't as if I were attempting to insinuate myself past an attentive guard-post, or negotiate the crossing of a mountain stream, or climb over a steep wall that had broken bottles all along its top, after taking care that no one was looking; I was merely walking along one of the main thoroughfares and on a route taken by a great many buses on their way out of the town. Nevertheless, part of the attraction was the sheer distance – it was a matter of going to the far end of the town – and the offer of a choice of itineraries: not much of a choice, it is true: there were two, with a third which was a slight variant of the second. One could head straight up by the Five Ways, the second-hand bookshop near the top, and the ugly motor show-rooms, and then cross over onto the main road to Southborough; or, more agreeably, one could loop round the edge of the Common, past the doctor's red house with the long garden, Thackeray's house, the big tea place with the pretty cast-iron green balconies on the corner, then over, past Grabban's antique shop, the new hospital, past Florian, the home of my Limbury-Buse cousins. For the house was a bit further up, beyond the monument to Canon Hoare and the invariable limits of the two Limbury-Buse itineraries – neither Geoff nor his father would have ever been aware of the existence of the house, and they were far from being alone in this respect; it was not the sort of place that one would have noticed, had one not known in advance where to find it: on the left side of the main road, almost opposite St John's church; at least, I think it was, for one could not see the church from the ground-floor window.

A possible variant would be to take the first route, up Mount Pleasant and as far as the Five Ways, then cut off to the left, at the big Public Convenience. This would bring me into the little, unpretentious street that contained the old Public Library. I was fond of the old Public Library, which was just a three-storeyed house, 1890 or 1900 or thereabouts, like all the other houses in the street, and that had been singled out for semi-disgrace, assigned to the role of public building. I don't know what the house had done to merit what certainly could be seen as a demotion, removing it from the unassuming, but respectable, fraternity of its neighbours, most of them small family houses, though two of them contained fairly unprestigious dental surgeries, and one, on its ground-floor, in a panel shaped as a half-circle over the white-painted front-door, announced itself, bizarrely as I thought, as the local branch of the Oddfellows. Even the Oddfellows had lace curtains; only the Public Library had a sort of black gauze in its ground-floor windows, with PUBLIC LIBRARY in flaking gold on each. Perhaps the house had been punished as a result of some minor scandal that had taken place on one of the upper storeys and that had been observed from a similar level from across the street, which was narrow, though not demeaningly so. You had to go down behind the old Town Hall to discover the existence of *really* narrow streets. This one was still asserting a justified claim to respectability.

Certainly Public Libraries must have come pretty low in municipal priorities – well below Public Conveniences for both sexes, the most luxurious of these, in George V style, had replaced, sometime in the

1930s, the little cottage in Kentish clapboard, the front painted white, the sides painted black, *Fonthill*, in which we had lived on coming to Tunbridge Wells for good in 1921. The big pale beige Convenience was situated on the edge of the Common, where it faced, discreetly, but still very visibly, onto the back of the Pantiles. Such priorities would have certainly been observed in a middle-class town where it would be assumed that the reading public would either buy books, from Goulden & Currey, or would borrow them from the two circulating libraries provided by Boot's and Smith's.

There was something rather attractive about the undramatic and very ordinary shabbiness of the place and by its modest concern not to call attention to itself nor to advertise its no doubt meagre wares. The entrance downstairs was very dark, but fairly clean, in so far as one could see; but the shabbiness really took over on the stairs, and seemed to thrive more and more at each step up, the peeling wallpaper showing extending continents of dark damp; and it established a seedy mastery in the front room on the first floor, which doubled up as Reading Room – written in black letters on the glazed glass door: RE DIN   ROOM [the A and the G having apparently fallen out in despair] – and dusty museum displaying cases of stuffed birds (that may have been among the earlier, juvenile, more tentative works of R. Septimus Gardiner), glass-fronted boxes of faded, pinned-down butterflies, and fossils dug out of the sand by the Wellington Rocks.

The four windows onto the street which did not open – the cords hung down sadly towards the chocolate-painted floorboards, suggestive of patches of dark dried blood, like spent hangman's ropes – were so dirty that they offered no clear view of the street below; and in the winter there was a little asthmatic fire in the grate that gave off much more smoke than heat. Against the far wall there was a high glass-fronted book-case that did not open and that contained odd numbers of Whitaker's Almanack dating back to the 1890s. On the landing there was another door that I managed to push open against some resistance from within and that gave on to a much smaller room that faced onto what once had been a tiny garden, and that was now overrun with willow herb. The room was crammed full of broken bits of furniture, chairs with the horsehair falling out, the remains of an iron bedstead, tables with their legs missing, a teapot with its spout broken off and its top gone astray. There were the remains of a wallpaper in purple flowers, the damp marks competing with those of the staircase to form moonlike seas and continents. I liked to think that I was the only one who knew of the existence of the abandoned backroom.

There was a regular clientèle of poorly dressed male and female readers – though two of them could hardly qualify for that rather grand title, for I never caught them in the act of reading, they just stared sightlessly ahead of them – the former sitting in their dirty macs, wheezing, expectorating, picking their noses or their teeth, or both, and talking to themselves in a regular low murmur. The women were quieter, though there was one, very hunched and tiny, who made high-pitched whistling sucking noises, the origins of which could be traced to oblong paper packages, like tiny bolsters, in bright yellow, and bearing letters in bright red, and that contained evil-looking black coils of liquorice. I quite often stopped there, to take a look at the papers which we did not get at home, and to read the *Connoisseur* and the *Studio*, which, apart from myself, did not seem to be very much in demand, though the liquorice lady would linger for hours over the *Field* and the *Sporting Life*. It was no use trying to get hold of the *Daily Telegraph*, which was regularly monopolized by one of the men – I suppose he made a grab for it as soon as the place opened in the morning – who would not relinquish it till he had finished the crossword, and this would take him much of the day.

Very occasionally I would look in in the morning, before my eleven o'clock drink in the pub that was in a small building that must have at one time been the stables of the Calverley Hotel and that was now mostly used by the waiters and domestic staff of the place when they were off-duty, and by a wonderfully talkative lady in a changeless and somewhat greasy black velvet toque called *Maud*. Maud seemed as permanent a fixture of the single-roomed pub as were the 'readers' of the room up on the first floor. But, more often, I would stop off there in the early afternoon, on my way to the top end of the town. Very rarely, I would look in in the evening, on my way back. I think most of them – the number varied from ten to a dozen – must have stayed there throughout the opening hours. In the afternoons, there would be empty, greasy-looking paper bags in front of their places on the three long tables, the remains, I suppose, of whatever they had brought with them for lunch. Life upstairs in the Reading Room had a reassuring immobility about it, very much in contrast to the bustle and noise of the ground-floor, with people coming and going, women and small children, I suppose from the unknown areas behind the old Town Hall, handing in books and taking out new ones. Although the Reading Room stocked *Modern Boy*, *Beano*, the *Children's Newspaper*, and whatever weeklies or monthlies addressed themselves to schoolgirls, I never saw any children, whether in the uniforms of one of the local schools, or dressed more casually, in the room upstairs. Perhaps, at some previous time, one or two had ventured up there and had been frozen out by the angry stares of the regulars, who certainly did not look as if they had had any children of their own or would have had much time for children in a general sense. Even I, in my twenties, could feel the unspoken disapproval of their glances; it was pretty clear that I was much too young to gain proper admittance, as a full-paid-up member, to a wonderfully poor and shabby version of a very exclusive club. Or it may have been that I was too well-dressed and was seen as letting down the high standards of frayed shabbiness that was expected of anyone seen regularly up there. But habit wears down most such unwritten and unspoken rules, and, in the course of time, I could feel myself being granted a rather grudging acceptance despite my clothes and my youthful appearance. After a time, two of the regular male readers, both senior members, judging from their seats – one next to the window, the other with his back to the spluttering fire – even gave me a look of recognition: a very slight concession to a timid sociability. Of course, in such a place, there could be no question of anyone actually *greeting* anyone else, and though, as I have said, there was a regular, even, low buzz of conversation, it was entirely self-addressed. Now and then individual words and exclamations could be distinguished: *Well, I never, Blow me down!*, *Who would have thought it!*, *Utterly disgraceful!* (a literary intrusion, possibly), and, once, in a very upperclass voice, *By Jove!* indicating, like the *utterly*, that the club seemed to offer a pretty wide social range. It even occurred to me that the *By Jove!* reader might have been one of the six local hermits. The nearest thing to a conventional conversational exchange was when the liquorice lady caused a shocked temporary silence among the steadily low-pitched droners by saying quite distinctly, and in very broad Kent: *Shut up!* This was clearly an appalling breach of decorum; but it was the only time that I heard anything of the kind. The series of low-pitched drones soon picked up again, like the steady hum of machinery. The incident had presumably been forgotten and forgiven. There was a notice, in black letters on a washable white – not *very* white – background, over the glass-fronted book-case, marked with the word SILENCE. I took this to mean – and so presumably did my seniors – that this signified not talking to anyone else. The steady low drone was really part of the silence, like the popping hum of a gas-fire or the smooth murmur of a generator.

In the (relatively) silent upstairs ark of literacy, or apparently affected illiteracy (I am referring to the sturdy minority of two or three non-readers), one had to be rather careful where one sat. The places by the window were occupied, winter and summer, by the more resolute regulars, so were those nearest to the sad little fire (even when it wasn't lit, I suppose simply to indicate a long-established right). There were generally a few free places further in and at the middle table which caught the through draught of the door every time someone came in or went out. But it was advisable to check on the seat before actually sitting down on the bare wood. I still remember the slight shock of coming into contact with something that was both soft, squelchy and rather moist: I had placed myself on top of a brown paper-bag of rockfish that the liquorice lady had purchased for her cat. Fortunately, she had been too engrossed in the current issue of *Country Life* to have noticed what had happened, and I had been able to move down one place without having been detected, after wiping the seat of my grey flannels, though I had retained the feeling of dampness in my left buttock. Up till this incident, I had rather wondered why one of the masculine readers had been in the habit of bringing with him his own clearly much-used and heavily stained chintzed cushion in a still just discernible pattern of blue and purple flowers and pale green leaves. I had assumed from this self-indulgence that he either had a tendency to boils or to piles (though I have never discovered just what that unpleasant-sounding malady consisted of) or that the cushion was his over-demonstrative manner of setting out his claim to his usual seat.

After a few weeks, the 'readers' did not even look up when, after coming in and taking a paper or a magazine from the rack, I sat down at the middle table. Their indifference gave me an agreeable feeling of 'belonging'. I had been accepted by this disparate company, just as I had been accepted by Maud and the impressive-looking Head Waiter at the little pub attached to the Calverley. What made the feeling all the more agreeable was the certitude that none of my mother's friends, nor indeed any of my own, would have known even of the existence of the ordinary-looking little house, much less of the rather mysterious group of people who were in the habit of sitting through much of the day upstairs. It was rather like being a member of a secret society – the destiny, perhaps, of this eminently unnoticeable road that housed, a few doors down, the Oddfellows. They – the Oddfellows, I mean – must have been a different lot, however, from my companions, who did not look as if they had ever belonged to anything (though two of the men wore silver British Legion badges in their shiny lapels, the badges did not seem to form much of a bond between the two of them, for they always sat far apart, and never gave one another as much as a glance). I have always been attracted to the seedy fraternity of small provincial Public Libraries, wondering where the regulars came from, where they slept – in this instance, some looked as if they had made a habit of sleeping on the Common. Sometimes I was tempted to wait on till the place closed, in order to see if any of them went off together – or in which direction they headed. But I never did.

I did not want to find out too much; it was as well to leave at least one small area of mystery, just as it would no doubt have been a mistake actually to have succeeded in tracking down the anonymous, drooping, woebegone seller of the *Evening Argus*, in his dispirited vigil outside the Great Hall Cinema. It was enough to see them there day after day and to know that their presence could be relied upon. Sometimes I wondered what they did with their Sundays; but, of course, there was no means of knowing. Had I frequented the room long enough – a matter of several years – I would no doubt have noticed first one absence, then another, attributable perhaps to illness or to death. But a longer period was denied me. Almost without warning – though first the building site, following the sudden demolition of the elegant row of fine stone Decimus Burton houses stretching from opposite Lloyd's Bank almost to the level of the Calverley, should have been a danger signal – the little community of self-mutterers was all at once dispersed, scattered goodness knows whither, never to be encountered again. In my many walks to the upper end of the town, I never caught so much as a glimpse of any of them. The building of the hideous new Town Hall complex, a year or two before the outbreak of the Second World War, included a very modern, spacious new Public Library, together with a lecture room, a picture gallery, and a municipal museum. The new Library was a very clinical affair, spotless, with concealed lighting and a series of little polished tables scattered over the vast room. It was clearly too much for the old gang, who would have felt altogether out of place in such a functional atmosphere. Anyhow, I never saw any of them there; and I never tarried there myself. The unassuming little house in the side street was closed up, its ground-floor windows were boarded over; there did not seem any plan of assigning the house back to some private activity, so as to put it once more in line with all its neighbours in the road. The letters PUBLIC LIBRARY long remained faintly visible over the locked and bolted front-door; and there were dirty yellowish blinds pulled down over the four windows of the first floor. I even tried the place from the back and noticed that the window of the little room in which the broken furniture had been stored had been boarded up. I don't know what eventually became of the place, I did not want to know, henceforth avoiding that particular route, now that it had lost its charm as a stopping place, an upper room in which to linger and to take regular dips of reassurance, even, in its modest way, a sort of Home from Home. Perhaps it too was demolished and replaced by a petrol station, or converted into flats. I looked in the smart new Museum; there was a whole section on Tunbridge ware, but the stuffed birds, the fragile, fading butterflies and the fossils had been denied places there. Like the regulars, my unknown, but not indifferent companions, of a few mornings and of many afternoons, they had disappeared without a trace.

In my account I have lingered so long at the Old Public Library – as long almost as I used to stop off there in transit, on my way up or down – that it might be thought that I had actually lost sight of my ultimate destination on the long pull up to the far end of the town. But I am not likely ever to forget Percy House, or why I went there pretty well every afternoon that I was in Tunbridge Wells over a period I suppose of something like ten or fifteen years. Apart from providing me with what amounted to a second home – the old Public Library being more in the nature of an agreeable waiting-room, a breathing-space – spacious, delightfully untidy, rather mysterious, with its shuttered and unused rooms, and the exploration of a varied, tulgy garden, and offering me the excitement and anticipation of a choice of new itineraries, it gave me someone to talk to – or rather to listen to – on a whole range of subjects that would otherwise have been unlikely to have been touched upon by the much-travelled Major Moreland and his regular cronies at his junk-shop near the Central Station, or by Mr Rayward, the man with a black patch over his left eye, and always dressed in a three-piece blue suit with a thin chalk stripe, who ran the book section of Goulden & Currey's upstairs – another of my favourite stopping-places – who was a great deflator of the locally pretentious.

Percy House opened up to me a number of entirely unfamiliar worlds, as widely diversified and as generally unrelated as the London music-hall in its heyday before 1914, the London chess-playing coffee-houses that were the habitual meeting-places of the varied subjects of the old Habsburg Empire at much the same period, and student life in Hamburg and Berlin in the 1890s. Of course I was almost alone in the secret knowledge of the existence of this exotic enclave on the road to Southborough; and it was towards this unfamiliar territory that I stepped so eagerly and regularly up one or other of the hills on so many afternoons in the late thirties and throughout much of the forties.

Percy House was the home of my sister's future in-laws, Mr and Mrs Frank Papé, their son Lionel, an only child, and the fourth member of the household, Miss Everitt (I never heard her addressed otherwise, she was one of those people who just seemed never to have run to the intimacy of a Christian name, all her paintings were signed, with characteristic discretion: 'E. Everitt'. There was a discretion, too, about her actual status in the household. She had been the closest friend of Mrs Papé's from their student days at the Slade, so that an outsider might have been tempted to describe her as a 'companion'.) Frank Papé and his wife were book-illustrators and artists. They represented what seemed to be an ideal working partnership: Frank did the outlines and put in all the minute details, his wife then added in the colours. She also wrote the text of a number of children's books, while her husband provided the illustrations in black and white: the partnership operating in reverse. Miss Everitt was also a painter and a water-colourist, but she worked on her own and did not seek to find a market for her work.

When I first got to know them – I suppose in 1936 or 1937, when Lionel and my sister, Diana, were already engaged, they had been in the house for about seven or eight years, though, to judge from the general state of the place, it looked as if they had been in occupation much longer. For the house somehow matched – quite unintention- ally – its peculiar jumble of furniture: ricketty tables covered with heavy woollen cloths, chairs with their backs falling off, corner cupboards that were having difficulties in holding on to their chosen corners, and half-forgotten pieces of considerable value, left in semi- disgrace, banished to dark recesses in rooms that were no longer used – as I shall suggest, most of the leisure life of the house was confined to a single, very dark room to the right of the entrance-hall – with an equally crowded store-room of miscellaneous items of ill-assorted and unexpected knowledge, memory, and experience. I would come to expect many references to the boisterous and often violent alcohol- ism of pre-war London, a place that went on drinking right through the day and much of the night, and rather nostalgic evocations of the bright glare of gaslight that contributed to the sheer vigour and gusto with which leisure had been conducted, almost as if time had been running out (as, indeed, it did). Another lost world that, under such expert guidance, I loved exploring, and one in which annual Fairy Books, Blue, Red, Golden and Ruby, grew fatter and fatter, as if the demand for these little winged creatures, at least among the self- assured, confident middle-classes, had been inexhaustible, enabling book-illustrators to lead quite prosperous lives, to inhabit large houses in Surbiton, and even to run to the modest luxury of having living-in servants and nannies.

The house then was a mirror held up to the lost glories and to the comfortable optimism of a pre-1914 world. But the 1920s were further represented by descriptions of encounters, in top London hotels, with American tycoons who had literary pretentions, one of them the millionaire Charles Bedeaux, later the extremely dubious friend of the Duke and Duchess of Windsor, who, in the immensity of his conceit, had at one time contemplated writing his memoirs – or hiring someone to write them for him – and then getting them suitably, that is to say, lavishly, and in the decadent style of fifteen or twenty years back, illustrated. The project never got beyond one or two splendid meals at the Ritz, and wonderful promises that never materialized, though some of the work had actually been done and delivered. Another patron who did at least produce the goods was the strangely self-indulgent – no doubt he could afford to be – American novelist, James Branch Cabell, a sort of pre-Tolkien or C. S. Lewis of the twenties and the early thirties, who had managed to convince himself – and he had his devotees too among a rather committed, even fanatical, group of readers – that Tunbridge Wells and its surrounding district, High Brooms, Hawkenbury and Southborough presumably included, would provide a suitable setting for a whimsical, mock-medieval never-never land, *Poictesme* (in Ye Oldie French), in which acts of chivalry were everyday occurrences in the whole area covered by the green *Maidstone & District* buses and in which slender feminine white arms holding shining swords projected themselves from the middle of deep black lakes; I suppose a role was even found to accommodate the reed-clogged Brighton Lake, on the edge of the Common and facing onto the red-brick façade of the West Station. Tunbridge Wells, till then almost entirely waterless, save for the brackish yellow stuff that came out of the chalybeate spring at the side of Boots, in the Pantiles, in its new capacity as capital of *Poictesme*, was even accorded the benefit of a clear, winding river that divided the town between its two lush banks. It was certainly one of the stranger fates to have been imposed, from across the Atlantic, on the quiet little middle-class place, most of the inhabitants of which – my mother included – would certainly never have heard of Mr

Cabell. But, unlike the rascally Bedeaux, he had at least paid – and paid handsomely – for the bizarre, wilting illustrations that accompanied – and, indeed, suited – his chronicles of pseudo-medieval daring-do and that, probably, more than anything else, helped establish Frank Papé's reputation as a book-illustrator on both sides of the Atlantic. Like the salmon-teaming rivers of bucolic *Poictesme*, the Cabell books carried its illustrator on a swiftly-flowing stream: seven books between 1921 and 1930: 1921, 1923, 1925, 1927, 1928, 1929, 1930. Then the flow had stopped abruptly. Perhaps the author had died, or maybe he had tired of fantasy. Still, such a run of orders must have helped to keep the wolf from the door and to have tided the embattled household over what must have looked like being the most difficult post-war years. Only Anatole France during the same decade had been as generous a provider. In both cases, there was a matching of minds and of styles, both authors getting the illustrator that they most deserved. Indeed, I cannot help thinking that *Poictesme* may have had something to do with the decision to take on Percy House.

There was a less exalted, but, in the end, more profitable, because much longer-lasting, transatlantic outlet for the works produced in an upstairs room – Frank and his wife shared a studio, so that they could work together – in the house, in the form of the weekly strip-illustrations, depicting historical scenes, for 'Uncle Ray's Column' in the *Cleveland Plaindealer*. The strip ran from the twenties, through the thirties, forties and fifties and just into the sixties, a merciful source of regular income during a period in which book-illustrating, especially in wood-cut or pen-and-ink, had shrivelled miserably. 'Uncle Ray' (Ramon Coffman) seemed pleased enough with his weekly provision of neat little pictures in firm outline; he was also, I think, a cousin of the illustrator. Frank and his wife had succeeded in adjusting themselves to change and to the demands of a very different market, in the harsh post-war years that cannot have had very much to offer three former students of the Slade who had done their training there in the 1900s. Children's strip-cartoons, however educationally uplifting, were certainly a bit of a let-down after the solid glories of the big annual Fairy Books (the last, timid straggler among these, the *Ruby Fairy Book*, had come out in 1922), or even the strange gothick fantasies of *Poictesme*.

What must also have seemed a let-down, both in the post-war years and during the war itself, was teaching art, drawing, painting, and perspective at a large prep school, Newlands, run by another relative. Mrs Papé had started teaching at Newlands in 1915 or 1916, and Lionel had spent seven (fairly miserable) years there as a pupil. I don't think his mother had had to pay any school fees and this would of course have been known to all the other boys. After the war, she had carried on teaching there part-time. This would mean having to stay over a couple of nights in the middle of each week. Genteel poverty had to keep going somehow, there had been no war gratuities for book-illustrators back with dysentery from the Greco-Bulgarian front, and , returning, after four years, to discover that such openings as had remained in the now much more restricted field of book illustration had gone elsewhere to those available on the spot. It was quite an achievement to have succeeded in keeping going at all: an admirable example of middle-class resilience and toughness, and the ability to make discreet use of an extended family network.

The house itself gave no visible outward hint of so much European, Edwardian and transatlantic experience; and I was glad of this, for it managed to retain its air of mystery in face of the general public, and I did not want any stranger, any passer-by to be let into the secret. In fact it did not give a hint of anything very much, for it was very difficult to see from the road, apart from the words PERCY HOUSE, written in flaking black letters, on two greyish pillars that had at one time supported the front-gate, on a pale beige background surrounded by a thick black border, as if the very name had been in mourning; and the lettering was itself so dilapidated that the two pillars might have simply been indicating a ruin, or the site of a big house that no longer existed, so heavily was the place screened by trees and shrubs that had grown up unchecked in the front.

If one did attempt to look through the shrubbery and the thick undergrowth, then one would gain rather more than a hint of neglect and decay. It looked – and was – very damp. Much of the guttering had fallen down. The porch and the entry appeared to be engaged in a losing battle with the serpentine coils of ivy and Virginia creeper that were clearly already more than a match for the powdering grey and sandy stonework. If one pushed one's way into the dark drive, itself disappearing beneath the invading vegetation – no vehicle had been that way for years, by the look of it – one would have a confused glimpse of the long façade of a house in grey stone marked by uneven blotches of black, dark green, pale brown and greenish yellow. It had once been a grey house, but now it had broken out into a more varied, though muted, palette: not bright colours, but the sad colours of damp and mould. There were brown and whitish fungi on the upper walls, below the level of a roof that was in the process of shedding many of its tiles. There was a thin layer of broken tiles among the other debris – including what looked like the remains of the front-gate – that helped to render indistinct the actual course of the drive and where the flower-beds had once been. It was still an imposing house, built to the demanding pretentions of a mid-Victorian upper-middle-class family, but it had seen better days. It was rather inviting and friendly in its very dilapidation, as if it did not care any more, had given up the struggle to present an impressive appearance. One of the stained-glass windows of the panels in the upper part of the front-door had been broken, the front-door itself did not shut properly, remaining semi-jammed all through the night. It was not a suspicious house.

Inside it was very dark, save in the hall, a longish corridor that ran the full length from the front-door to the back one, which, likewise being always open, and leading onto the big, semi-wild garden, was always quite light in the daytime. Dead leaves tended to blow in thickly into this corridor, a position that they would manage to retain until they were succeeded, though not entirely displaced, by a further layer of younger leaves with the beginning of the autumn gales. Apart from the scurrying leaves, the corridor also displayed relics of past luxuries: odd pieces of what had once been a croquet set, tennis rackets with broken strings, rusty garden tools, a lawn-roller, a little can on wheels once used for marking out the tennis-court, a hat-stand with a wide range of old hats, including two yellow panamas and a faded homburg. The overgrown windows of the dining-room, which was to the right of the hall, let in but little light, so that one banged constantly against large pieces of furniture, almost as invasive as the enveloping vegetation as it moved in on the inside from the outside. Furniture and vegetation seemed to be running neck and neck as to which would engulf the fabric of the house first. Some of the furniture, in so far as it could be picked out at all clearly, seemed to be of considerable value, though in a poor state of repair. There was a handsome oblong dining-room table in a warm, pinkish wood, but most of it was hidden under a coarse, shaggy cover with tassels at the edges. The table, which occupied most of the room, apart from an enormous, very dark Welsh dresser that stood against the far wall, was the principal focus of discussion, argument and exchange both during tea and at times when no food was being served. I very much liked their habit of sitting at table, a habit that I had come to appreciate while in France. The chairs placed around the table were relics of several sets, and offered a treacherous security, especially to the back. Over the black marble mantelpiece, there hung a big, darkish painting – in dark browns, sombre greys and night blues, with one or two touches of vivid red – representing the principal street of a village in North Wales, with geese, showing up a ghostly white against the dull and apparently stormy background, scattering in the path of a horse and cart, the whole thing in menacing colours that seemed to accentuate the muted tones prevailing in the room.

Despite the gloom, it was a friendly, welcoming room which would suddenly acquire a real glow of warmth and softened colour when the big central, light, covered in a pink shade with dangling pompoms at the edges, and which hung very low over the centre of the table, was turned on, generally quite a bit after whatever daylight had ever managed to penetrate the place had started to fade altogether, as if those sitting round the table found comfort in the silent, gentle approach of enveloping darkness. The seating – plan – if that was the right word for something that clearly had been established years before, as the result of some unspoken convention – was invariable; as a newcomer, I always sat with my back to the window facing onto the drive, rather as if I were being subjected to the scrutiny of an examination board of three. Actually it would never have occurred to me to have tried to sit anywhere else, for that was the only chair that was both free and relatively safe on that side of the table. Opposite me, on the far side, and with their backs to the fireplace – a popping gas-fire in winter – sat my three judges, each in his or her place, with seniority rightly going to the male figure in the middle, Frank. He was the one who did most of the talking and questioning and who seemed best at listening, always with an expression of more than polite interest, often as he toyed with the bowl of his empty pipe, or putting it between his teeth, making sucking noises. Frank's face, and those of his wife, to his left, and of Miss Everitt, to his right, and nearest the door – she always placed herself prudently near the door – were rather indistinct, with heavy areas of shadow below the eyes, the cheek-bones and the chins, in the fitful swaying light that came from the flickering gas-fire and from the gently circling central shade, its bobbles appearing in shadow to move slowly over the thick cloth that covered the table, as it registered the many currents of draught that came through the heavy curtains and the ill-fitting windows and beneath the door leading to the hall, so that the room seemed to be breathing in an irregular and silent rhythm. Mrs Papé never had very much to say, and, even if she had, it would have been quite hard for her to have got in a word edgeways; but she looked benevolent, her face floating above the table like an indistinct but friendly moon. It was as if they too, like the geese, had formed the subject of another sombre, rather formal composition, a difficult exercise in competing depths of shade, a challenge to the virtuoso of the yellow Hartmuth pencil, the whole range from HH to BB.

It was not a permanent panel of three. More often than not, at least at the time of my arrival, there would only be Frank and his wife sitting beneath the sombre tapestry of the ducks, Miss Everitt creeping in silently, almost apologetically, slightly bowed, and with her perpetual timid smile, at the precise moment at which the big teapot had been brought in from the scullery. But there was no hint of threat in this dark tableau, the three figures, once Miss Everitt had taken her seat near the door, were not judges, nor was I about to be judged. It was much more like a committee meeting that had for some reason been interrupted, and the proceedings of which were now about to be resumed: an impression substantiated by the presence, on the far side of the table, and to the right of the middle seat occupied by Frank, of a little brass bell that looked as if it had been of Alpine origin.

And indeed things did generally start just at the point at which they had been abandoned at the end of my previous visit, as I was asked, by one of them, what I had been up to since the last time that I had been there. Had I been writing any more short stories or articles for magazines? Had I brought any along to read to them? Or one of them might ask me if I had read anything interesting in the papers. But they seemed generally even more interested in my doings, even to the extent of wanting to know by which route I had come and whether I had stopped off at the Public Library. There would have been no point at all in my asking *them* questions of this kind, for I would know *exactly* what they had been doing, all three of them: Monday, the strip drawings would have to be posted off to Ohio in order to meet Uncle Ray's syndicated schedule; midweek, Mrs Papé would have been off on her usual trip to Newlands, Seaford, if it were term-time, and Friday she would be back. If my visit were on a Wednesday or a Sunday, Frank would have been on his bi-weekly visit to the chess club, which met in an upstairs room in a little café in Vale Road, near the corner, as it ran steeply down from the road-bridge over the railway-line. I never found out very much about the little chess club, save that, for some reason, it had been demoted, having previously met in a room in a house on Mount Ephraim, and having been expelled from the heights, to come and seek refuge in the room above the café, nor about those who attended it twice a week. He was strangely reticent about these to me mysterious fellow-players. I believe this was one of the rare cases when he liked to hold on to a small pocket handkerchief of anonymity. Anyhow, I never pressed him on the subject, being content mostly to let him do the talking. I would know too that Miss Everitt had not been out of the house, apart from pottering round the gardens at the back with a pair of secateurs if the weather had been inviting. She kept a shallow gardening-basket, a pair of old yellow gloves, some gardening tools, and a battered brown felt hat in the long hall, ready to hand for these occasional forays into the extensive and exciting territory provided by a garden that, apart from an old tennis-court, now visible only in outline, and no longer very level, also included a rich herb garden, a series of frames for strawberries, tomatoes, peaches and nectarines, many of them broken, a spreading mulberry, a weeping willow, a medlar, a huge copper beach, and a long deep orchard, the bitter apples lying rotting and severely pecked on the ground. There were also the remains of a rockery. The garden, rather like the house, seemed to have grown tired and to be giving up, a fading monument to lost ambitions.

I think it was this sense of failure, of high ambitions abandoned, that made the unkempt garden so attractive to me, in its increasing wildness and lack of order. It certainly did manage to offer a wonderfully varied geography out in the open and I suppose what remained of the conservatory, with its half-dead vine and still surviving orange trees in little green boxes could add a continent or two, as well as the reminder of a lingering, somewhat pinched and frozen exoticism, even tropicality. I don't think Miss Everitt ever went out into the overgrown front, too exposed to observation from the busy road, not a secret place like the series of gardens at the back, and she had certainly not set foot beyond the limit of the one-time, now purely notional, gate into the equally notional drive, for a number of years. She seemed to have no friends in the town, nor regret their absence, and she appeared to have no relatives anywhere else. Her only other concession to a timid mobility was to come downstairs at tea-time, something of a token gesture to a restricted sociability, for she would go up again round about six, and would remain up there for her supper.

So there was something entirely reassuring about the predictability of their movements – or lack of them – throughout the week and even on Sundays, a day that was not accorded any special treatment. Perhaps, in the distant years before 1914, or again in the 1920s of recovered mobility, the three of them had grown tired of travelling through Europe, leasing, for one season, a chalet in the Tyrol, spending a few months on the Italian Lakes, moving house once more to a farm in Tuscany, then switching northwards, to linger perhaps for a whole year in a rustic black-and-white cottage set in the depths of the Black Forest.

The Slade, back sometime in the early-1900s, had no doubt imposed an artistic itinerary of Alpine mountain and waterfall – Frank's grandfather, family tradition would have it, had eventually lost his sight as a result of too long a contemplation of these, the sun glinting through their silver spray – of gentle Tuscan landscape, abrupt ochre hills with ruined towers and crenellations and creeping vines, of alarming Grimm-like Germanic forest, of reddish, jagged Dolomite: a topography that drew mostly on the Central Powers and on Northern Italy, but that totally – and oddly – ignored France, at least in the case of Frank and his wife, if not of the third member of the household. Or perhaps such frontiers had been recommended not so much by the Slade, which would presumably have found room too at least for the Ile-de-France, the Valley of the Loire, and the Normandy coast and estuaries – but by current pre-1914 circuits of travel in the High Age of Baedeker and that seemed heavily to have favoured the baroque and the bulbous; or these may have been due to the personal choice of one who had grown up initially in Hamburg and in Berlin. Anyhow, for a few years, they had returned to their pre-war itineraries – it may have had something to do with harking back to the time when all three had been young, wide-eyed enthusiasts, just out of Art school, and earnestly engaged on the Grand Tour that had then been most in favour with the current artistic orthodoxies; or it may merely have had something to do with less exalted considerations, in the conditions of the early 1920s especially: the opportunity to take full advantage of an exchange rate so favourable as to make leading a wandering existence through Austria and Germany much cheaper than living in England. Anyhow, at some stage in the twenties – since about 1908, the trio had become a foursome, so that, in the mid twenties, the question of schooling may have arisen, they had finally settled for less ambitious progresses; and certainly much less fatiguing ones, too, for their boxes of paints, their easels, their brushes, their tennis-rackets, their umbrellas, their parasols, their trunks, their hat-boxes, even their teapots and their tins of English tea, perhaps even the croquet set, then still intact, had gone along with them, or ahead of them, as they had trailed across the serrated face of Central Europe and Northern Italy.

First, they had taken furnished accommodation in the southern suburbs of London. The choice may have been dictated by a desire to recapture something of the Edwardian scale of their household in the immediate pre-1914 years, when plenty of money had been coming in from publishers – 1911, with four books, and, above all, 1912, with six – had been bumper years for Frank and his wife – and when they had been living in considerable style in an enormous house in Surbiton: billiard-room, breakfast-room, a winter garden and a conservatory, seven bedrooms, a tennis-court, a croquet lawn, a rock garden reached by a series of paved steps (the subject of one of Miss Everitt's tiny compositions), a vegetable garden. Then they had begun moving again, but this time more modestly, through the length and breadth of West Kent and East Sussex: first, a largish house on Southborough Common lent to them rent-free by a providential Dutch Jewish friend – perhaps a survivor from pre-1914 chess-playing activities in London *brasseries*. Then the same generous Dutchman had set them up in a converted oast-house somewhere down in the pretty little valley below Bidborough Ridge and near the line from Tonbridge to High Brooms. The oast-house had a strange round drawing-room – I had seen photographs of this and they had led me to wonder how they had managed to hang up their many compositions – three lots of them, signed FCP, AP, EE, representing three distinct schools of painting (though all of them the Slade) on the circular walls. Then there had been a cottage in the Den Country, followed by a large house on the edge of Ashdown Forest. Finally, in 1930 or in 1931, following no doubt the run of the seven Cabells, and the promise of more orders – a Tartarin, a Suetonius, a second Crusoe, a Lorna Doone, an Arabian Nights – from different publishers (not to mention Uncle Ray) – the calendar of the family fortunes or misfortunes seems to have borne little relation to that of the more public ups and downs of the world economy and of relations between the Powers (save in 1914 and in 1939) – they had all at once decided to come to rest and to stay put.

By the time I came to know them, they had been in Percy House for seven or eight years. What is more – contrary to the prevailing practice of the twenties and the thirties – they had *bought* the house. And with the house went the considerable tract of land behind it. They could certainly have done much worse than the untidy, chaotic and tumbling many-coloured house, full of draughts and damp, but extensive enough to provide wide areas of individual seclusion and specialised activity: somewhere upstairs, in parts that I had never visited, room must have been found for at least two separate studios and a work-room for Lionel. Judging from the mittens worn by my three friends at tea, the studio rooms must have been pretty arctic in winter. Certainly, their relative – and, in Miss Everitt's case, complete – immobility offered a restful contrast to many accounts of an exotic past, of sweltering Wilhelminian summers, of black and white Carinthian winters, of blazing Italian springs, and of a wonderfully picaresque existence no doubt better to listen to than to have experienced. (I sometimes wondered what the small boy must have made of all these bewildering migrations; certainly, later in life, once married and a father of four, he would set his face resolutely against not only any form of foreign travel, but any notions of holidays that involved movement, save that, predictable, imposed by industrial orders, within England itself.) At least such peregrinations provided the subject of many evocations of the two Empires in the last years of their glory and that I followed, with wrapt attention, in the changeless, shut-in, embattled dining-room.

So much then for the dining-room and the pretty wild-growing gardens to the back, the two places in which I spent most of my time while in my alternative home, one that, over a gap of more than ten years, had replaced the equally mysterious, equally dilapidated, St Leonard's House in the Hythe, down by the Colne and almost in sight of the red-sailed Danish barges. But I have not quite finished with the house. To the left of the hall, there was a long, bleak drawing-room that opened out onto the ruined conservatory and what had once been a bold attempt at a winter garden. The drawing-room had not been used for a number of years – I don't know just at what stage they had abandoned it for good, but, by the time of my arrival, parts of the ceiling were beginning to cave in, and the furniture was covered over in greying dust-sheets. Some of the best pieces may have been confined to the exile of falling plaster and tearful damp; but it was impossible to tell. One could make out the outline of a large sofa, of a set of high-backed chairs, of a grand-piano; and there was a ghostly round object that might have been a terrestrial globe (indicating, I would like to surmise, the old frontiers of a lost pre-1914 Europe). But the drawing-room was not a place to linger in; even with the wooden shutters permanently closed, it retained an icy cold.

But upstairs, to the right of the corridor on the first floor, there was a small enclave of neatness, tidiness, minute care, and miniature good taste: the little sitting-room of an Edwardian or late-Victorian gentlewoman in her youth, as much a mirror to a given period as the carefully reconstructed room of a museum, but this one living and lived in, and very welcoming. It was a delightful surprise in smallness, perfectly adjusted to the neat proportions of its resident. There was a tiny bureau in rosewood; against the window, partly obscured by virginia creeper, a small, very handsome dining-room table was covered by a white embroidered cloth. Three round tables with scallopped edges stood in the corners, above them glass-fronted corner-cupboards, firmly attached to the walls, asserting their full confidence in their respective occupancies. The floor was richly covered with three very worn but still brilliantly coloured bokhara rugs. The mantelpiece carried an array of china dogs, toby jugs, a silver travelling-clock, its silver surround in an embossed pattern as if it had been sprayed, ivory elephants in ascending order of size, and highly polished silver objects. On the walls there hung an assortment of very small, delicate water-colours, in fresh, bright colours, very clear-cut, and with firm outlines – some of these were in pen-and-wash – depicting such peaceful subjects as a sunny moorland of heather, a long white house that could have been a country rectory and that was surrounded by old trees, evergreens, yews, a bright herbaceous border, a sunlit meadow with cows grazing, a primrose wood, the estuary of a small river as it fanned out towards the sea, its mouth marked by a tall wooden pole aslant, tipped by a triangle covering. They were tiny pictures, placed very close together, full of light, and, in the evenings, the only time I was admitted, the room itself was very well lit from a series of table-lamps in light green silk that were reflected in enlarging green circles on the polished wood of the small tables. On the bureau there were three photographs in silver frames, two depicting a couple dressed in mid-Victorian style, the third of a small child in a white dress, holding a big hoop. Perhaps the first was that of Miss Everitt's parents, the little girl may have been herself. I never found out, not liking to ask. Nothing could have offered a greater contrast to the prevailing gloom of the dining-room and to the sombre colours of the big picture over the mantel-piece. In the winter there would always be a bright coal fire in the little grate, which was topped by a shining brass canopy. All the surfaces: tables, chair-backs, silver, brass, gleamed in the bright light; and the room smelt of wax polish. A door in the far wall led to the bedroom, and, possibly, the kitchen beyond.

The little sitting-room seemed to assert itself happily in its neat, immaculate independence like a small Swiss canton or a miniscule duchy that had got forgotten about in a surrounding empire of neglect. Much of its charm – apart from the evidence of loving care that it provided – was contained in the sheer surprise with which it confronted the privileged visitor, rather as if he had accidentally stumbled on a secret room, suddenly revealed in all its small perfection and completeness, at the light touch of a panel. The first time that I was admitted there I was too surprised to make any immediate comment. I could see her looking at me, with her usual kindly shy expression now giving hints of amusement, as if to say to me: 'You didn't expect this, did you? You would never have guessed'. Well, I suppose, come to think of it, I might have a bit, from the neatness of her clothes – all the year round she was dressed in brown autumnal tints, in heavy woollens or tweeds and very solid-looking brown walking-shoes; and, at the top of her buttoned-up dress, she wore a little camée, cream on a light brown background, depicting a lady with piled-up hair in profile. There was such a general symphony of browns as almost to give the impression of a special, very safely middle-class uniform, designed to order for an elderly and fairly high-ranking Girl Guide. Even in the hottest weather there was never any concession to summer, never any question of her switching from wool and tweed to silk and cotton.

I felt I was being let into a secret; and I was certainly being honoured. She generally invited me to come up there just as she was leaving the tea-table at about six. But the invitation was not just a matter of form; it was a rare privilege, not, I think, strictly or deliberately rationed, but spaced out in such a manner as to make my infrequent trips upstairs the more memorable. She would offer me a glass of sherry, giving me the choice of dry, very dry, or medium. And this was itself quite a ritual, involving the appearance of a polished silver tray, three decanters with silver labels on little chains round their necks and two sherry glasses with thick silver inlaid edges at the top. I would be invited to take a seat on a low chair covered in flowered cretonne and with short gilded legs like little golden hooves. One of the round tables, covered in a crocheted mat, would be placed beside me. And she would watch me attentively while I drank my glass. I would be offered another one, but no more after that.

Nearly always she particularly wanted me to talk about Paris, indicating that she had known the place quite well in the 1900s – she left the actual dates rather vague, 'sometime before the Great War' – when she had worked in one of the better-known *ateliers* of the rue Campagne-Première. No item of information could have surprised me more; it was difficult for me to come to terms with the presence in such an apparently improbable, even unsuitable, location of this slight, neat, brown-clad, middle-class, well-spoken Englishwoman. She seemed to belong by right to tea-parties on the lawn of a country house in the Home Counties. But, of course, with the inability of someone still in his mid or late twenties, I was unable mentally to allow for her own one-time youth and had momentarily forgotten, in the enclosed neatness of the little sitting-room, that she had met the other two at the Slade. Had she been to Paris first? Or had she for once broken up the trio to go off on her own? Maybe at one time she had even worn loose *moderne-style* clothes, heavily embroidered exotic caftans, vaporous flowing Japanese silks, a *bandeau*, and heavy jade ear-rings, and had daringly smoked a cigarette in black rice-paper in a long ivory holder. It was so hard to see back beyond the prevailing browns to a period when there might have been more colour in her life. I rather doubt, however, if there had ever been very much, at least as far as outward appearances and social attitudes were concerned. Frank had frequently held forth to me on the subject of the fecklessness and the immorality of artists; and his standards had always appeared to have been borrowed from Surbiton rather than from Chelsea. Having generally found it hard to make both ends meet, he had little sympathy for *la vie de bohême* and he liked to describe himself as a craftsman. It is true that there was a rather studied prurient naughtiness in some of his more elaborate work as an illustrator; but the prurience was very much reined in, a matter of hints and nudges rather than anything crudely explicit and it would have caused no offence to middle-class conventions of what was or was not proper: merely a mild titillation. Not for him the flowing cape, the unkempt beard, the Léon Blum wide-brimmed black hat and the loosely tied *lavalière*. His clothes were always conventionally middle-class, even professional: an old brown suit, a cardigan, in beige or grey wool, knitted by his wife, highly polished brown leather shoes, and, much of the year, grey woollen mittens. All three would generally be wearing these downstairs for tea and I presume that they wore them for work as well. His wife usually wore several thicknesses of woollen jerseys with abundant bobbles and her appearance suggested an active member of a Women's Institute or a kindly, patient lady who taught art and woodwork at a coastal prep school. It seems on the whole unlikely that Miss Everitt had ever come out in brighter colours. Though all three seem to have had little contact with the social life of Tunbridge Wells – Miss Everitt none at all, Mrs Papé only intermittently, between her trips to Seaford, and Frank only with the chess club (certainly not frequented by the Warwick Park, Molyneux Park or Frant Road set) and the Nevile Tennis Club – it was oddly appropriate that he should have done a picture book for the Oxford University Press about Warwick the Kingmaker, though I am not sure whether he would have made the connection, – their appearance would have been in perfect conformity with what was expected of the inhabitants of the little middle-class sanctuary: sensible, unostentatious, hard-wearing clothes. Even my mother, so censorious of the inhabitants of Percy House, could not have found anything to criticize in this respect.

During my visits upstairs, Miss Everitt would question me closely about Paris, displaying a minute knowledge of Montparnasse, the small streets off the Boulevard, and of the artists' studios in the *impasses* bordering the Avenue du Maine. She had little to say about her own life in the neighbourhood, apart from telling me the name of the painter under whom she had studied and who had been a minor figure in the group that exhibited at the *Salon des Indépendants*. But she would question me closely on my own activities in the city, how I spent my working day, where I went in the evenings, whether I spent them alone or in company, so that I had the impression that, while my own trips upstairs represented for myself timid plunges into the unexpected, my presence in her miniature sitting-room enabled her in some measure to follow me abroad and to retrace her own distant steps through once-familiar streets. Anyhow, as far as I was concerned, the strange house had acquired a new dimension and I had been given the additional advantage of a second home within a second home, a room in a dolls'-house, contained, like one of those squat Ukrainian toys in the shape of an egg, within a house of normal size.

The dining-room, the desolate, abandoned drawing-room, what was left of the once-proud conservatory, the spreading, uneven garden, and the occasional invitation upstairs were not quite the limits of the territory open to me within the place. Most of upstairs, including the rest of the first storey and the whole of the mysterious second was closed to me, and I would never have presumed to have explored in areas that could be expected to have held their own intimacies or to have indicated their sad barrenness. But, off the ground-floor corridor, on the right, its door partly blocked by the ruined croquet set, there was an old-fashioned lavatory with a wide, very comfortable, affluent-looking seat, designed to accommodate more generous proportions than those offered to sight, on these discreet occasions, by more recent generations, the veins of the rich old wood displaying interesting forms in various shades, like living organisms. The bowl too was fresh and welcoming, being decorated in a blue and white willow pattern design, now somewhat speckled. But what contributed to the uniqueness and surprise of the little room was the existence of its two windows: the one, glazed in pink glass, over the two panels of the door onto the corridor, the other, facing onto the garden, in mauve, red, green and gold stained-glass – not, as I recall, depicting a religious scene (a scourging of a bare back with thorns would have offered an interesting diversion) but just a bright jumble of colours, as if formed from the surviving fragments, in jagged, broken shapes, of a fourteenth-century church window of Flemish glass. Both seemed to underline the semi-devotional char-acter of the modest Temple of Ease spaced between the two positions of the windows as they were placed at right-angles one to the other and resulting in the diffused light coming from two different directions. If the afternoon sun were streaming in – and I would only be at my prolonged devotions there in the afternoon or early evening – and if there was a light breeze gently nudging the creaking branches of the old mulberry just outside the garden window, I would enjoy watching the moving coloured reflections, rather like transparencies, as they were filtered through the glass of the outer window and of the two panels of the door: pale pink, dark blue, very dark red, brilliant grass green, and a yellowish gold glow, as they crept up my lowered and unbuttoned trousers, stroking my bare legs and thighs, as if I had been transformed into a human kaleidescope of a whole spectrum of shifting colours. Apart from the gleaming and dancing stained-glass specks of light, as they moved aimlessly and caressingly over the lower parts of my body, swishing the walls like brightly coloured fireflies, and lighting up, in sudden shifting radiance, the three large spiders'-webs hanging from the ceiling, enriching the small clouds of dust raised by my feet with a luminosity of reds and greens, blues and yellows, so that the place of meditation seemed to be filled with swirling coloured clouds that grew brighter and more consistent with the setting of the sun, the little room offered abundant and unfamiliar reading material, quite beyond the scope both of Mr Rayward and of the Public Library, in the form of pages of the *Cleveland Plaindealer* that had been cut into rough squares and that were now doing their plain-dealing in a more humble capacity. But what I liked best there was the way the colours moved and swirled, lighting up the greyish, unwashed walls, giving strange and rapidly changing tints to the beams of dust as they rose lazily towards the festooned ceiling, and turning my hands all at once into succeeding shades of pink, red green, blue, and a pale gold.

In that strange house, nothing was quite as might have been expected, nothing could be taken for granted – an old barometer that hung in the corridor had sulked for years, refusing to look to the future, and pointing perpetually to CHANGE (a reasonably safe guess in any case), the black clock over the mantelpiece of the dining-room had as much lost interest in the march of time (the March of Time) as its mulish companion had in the weather – and this very lack of uniformity was part of the attractiveness of the house. A place in which everything had worked, as it were at the turn of a switch, would have been very dull; a place in which nothing had worked would have been pretty depressing, not to say unlivable in. Percy House had managed to achieve a sort of artistic and uneasy balance: some things worked, others didn't, and there would be an added satisfaction in knowing, as a result of constant experiment, which did and which didn't.

It is certainly symptomatic of the general unawareness in which so many residents of Tunbridge Wells have managed to remain of the very existence of the place that, while scores, in their letters to me, following the publication of my book, *Still Life*, could recall not only Florian, but also its five inhabitants (six if one includes the dog) even to the extent of remembering the nickname, 'Pussy', under which old Mr Limbury-Buse had been known both at home and to his closer friends at the club, not a single one has made any mention of Percy House or of its residents. Yet the house must have had a neighbour at least on one side (on the Southborough side it was flanked by the long line of the brick wall of a brewery), situated as it was on a busy road and in a built-up area. The house, like the little independent enclave on the first floor, seemed to have acquired a territorial autonomy that had placed it in a geographical vacuum, apparently removing it from being overlooked from any direction. Yet, at some earlier stage – certainly long before I had ever been aware of the place – it must have had quite frequent visitors, though no doubt not the sort of people that my mother or my aunt Emily would have thought worth knowing; there had been large tennis parties, important social occasions at which a potent homemade cider-cup had been served and thinly cut tomato sandwiches provided. But such reachings-out to an extended sociability had long been abandoned, they were not even mentioned in the course of my many visits. There remained just the geological evidence provided by the vague outline of the tennis-court. It is only recently that I have heard of these parties from my sister. At some stage in the thirties, the draw-bridges had been pulled up and the front-gate had been allowed to collapse.

The house and its owners had managed to sink into an oblivion so total that the thoughts of using it at least as a temporary bolt-hole to tide me over the more difficult war months that I had occasionally entertained, only to abandon them in the face of certain practical difficulties, seem in retrospect to have been based on almost perfect conditions of clandestinity. From some time in 1942, I was being harried by the State, in the form of beige OHMS envelopes in cheap, unsightly paper. For a time I had managed to remove myself from any direct contact with this insistent and unpleasant correspondence by keeping on the move from hotel to hotel, staying only short periods in each, well beyond the confines of Kent (I had been upgraded medically in Maidstone) and staying in succession in St Andrews, Carnoustie, Ripon, Nottingham, Blackpool. But I could not keep this evasive action up indefinitely, for one thing, it was getting more and more expensive, for another, I knew the beastly envelopes would catch up with me in the end, especially if I returned to my mother's. So what about Percy House? Certainly, no one outside would have had the slightest awareness of the existence of an extra resident.

But I had read too much about people who had sat it out, in secret rooms, in cellars, in attics, helped by members of their family, the entire length of the Spanish Civil War. I did not in fact ever attempt to go to ground at the top end of the town. I would not have thought of having been such an embarrassment to my three friends. Frank might have been tickled by the idea, but his wife would have regarded me, quite rightly, as a shirker. And my mother would have known about my hide-out and would have been too honest not to have revealed it to the authorities. I went home and waited for them to come, which they did, in the end. Still, I had gained some precious time. It had all been a fantasy; I had merely entertained the possible thought of a hidden refuge, in a vague, consoling sort of way, the usual dream about 'the little room over the sweet-shop'.

So much then for the potential role of Percy House as a physical, as well as a moral, refuge from the calls of collective orthodoxies and the tyrannies of the State. This would be to attach too much importance to a house that was not trying any more to prove *anything*, being merely content to go on providing the barest shelter against the fiercer of the elements (for it had positively *welcomed* in the damp). The wind was making steady advances up top, the drive offered plenty of evidence as to this, the other elements were making gradual inroads, as one outpost after another fell to them; and one would readily envisage the time when the first floor too would have to be evacuated – the warm, well-cared-for, welcoming enclave included (never was the saying 'being under the same roof' more graphically and alarmingly illustrated) – leaving the dining-room, the scullery, whatever served as a kitchen, and, so I hoped at least, my own little coloured shrine, as the remaining strongholds; for the outside was already silently, but implacably, gaining on the inside, as the corridor between front and back doors filled up with layer after layer of dead leaves, and as the two doors themselves, sweating and expanding with damp, proved less and less capable of carrying out their primitive functions of closing out the night, the rain, the cold, the wind and the odd intruder.

Indeed, I was present when what was left of the conservatory decided to give up, with a very modest, muted, discreet crash, barely audible, no powerful protest, more like a resigned sigh of tinkling glass and rotting wood too wet even to make a sharp crack, provoking, as the faintish, but no doubt long-awaited, sound reached the dining-room one windy autumn afternoon, an equally mild, unsurprised, simultaneous triple comment: 'that will be the conservatory', between mouthfuls of buttered toast spread with anchovy paste: not even a proper obituary; they did not even bother to get up and go and see the evidence of death, as it lay sprawling, amidst a tangle of former roof strops green with damp and broken panes of white-framed glass, on the left side of the house, leaving the abandoned drawing-room exposed at the far-end. Still, it did not do to try and look ahead. There was fight in the place as yet. And despite the impression – indeed the manifold evidence – of decline, it seemed a wonderfully happy house, in a casual, not-caring sort of way, though my mother would have been horrified by it – was in fact horrified by it the only time she went inside. She could never be induced to return a second time, always finding excuses, transmitted very half-heartedly by myself, and received as far as I could judge, with bland, polite, smiling – Frank especially could make the most charming smile give every hint of ironical disbelief – yet total incredulity: it was too long a pull up for her, and that sort of thing, perfectly unconvincing from one of the most energetic walkers, and one of the most stoutly and sensibly shoed in the whole of Tunbridge Wells. Anyhow, it soon came to be accepted – I imagine with a considerable measure of relief – that she would never be seen up there again, thus removing any need of some sort of further special effort, as well as the disruption of their normally easy-going time-table, in honour of her return. I don't think *any* visitor from outside – for I had soon achieved honorary insider status – would have been particularly welcome, my mother no doubt least of all.

But though she would never set foot in Percy House a second time, my mother never ceased to display an insistent, inquiring interest in its current state of neglect and advancing decay. She would ask me, on my return from each of my regular visits, whether anything else had fallen down, and on my saying that nothing else had, as far as I knew, she would seem a bit disappointed. The news of the quiet collapse of the pathetic remains of the conservatory left her meditative and uncharacteristically unquestioning for some weeks, as if to give herself time to digest the full impact of an event that must have seemed to her quite stupendous and full of allegorical significance, a local version *in petto* of *The Fall of the House of Usher*, though it had been received with such unruffled indifference by those most directly concerned. She seemed to think of the collapse of the conservatory as clear evidence of some sort of moral failing.

Generally, however, she would have to make do with questions that seemed banal, anyhow quite out of proportion to the scale of impending disaster to which she appeared to look forward with both certitude and, I think, a measure of grim self-satisfaction. Was anything ever *polished*? Were the tables ever *dusted*? Were the chair-covers ever *washed*? Did they even *have* any chair-covers? When had the windows last been *cleaned*? Were they going to get the front-door *repaired*, so that it would actually *shut*? My mother would ask, in the emphatic, *underlining* tone of voice that she reserved for routine cross-examinations as to my own rather indifferent attitudes to the accepted rules of personal domestic hygiene. I could not offer her very much satisfaction, making do with the rather feeble reply that, in the dim light – and even this she would take either as a sign of extreme parsimony, or as the result of a deliberate effort to cover up the visual evidence of months and years of past neglect, whereas, in fact, there was a much simpler explanation: Frank and his wife were in the habit of spending their long working-hours under unusually powerful acetylene pressure

lamps, he wearing a canvas eye-shade with a green interior, no doubt
borrowed from tennis, to protect his eyes from the bright glare, when
they were engaged on pen-and-ink, engraving or colouring, often in
minute detail, so that they would welcome the opportunity to rest
their eyes when they came downstairs – I had not noticed, though, of
course, I had. For I had all my mother's watchful concern for
minutiae, and could at once spot if any familiar object – such as the
little alpine cow-bell – had been missing or out of place. My mother
generally concluded my no doubt disappointing reports on the state
of play in the chaotic house up at the top of the hill by reminding me
that she had lit the boiler, pending my return from up there, and that
it might be a good idea, now that the water was piping hot, if I were to
have a *bath*.

As may readily be gathered from all this, she rather disapproved of
the four current inhabitants of Percy House and of what she had seen
and heard of their manner of life, though her disapproval would not
be measured out in equal proportions. For instance, she was quite
willing to find excuses for Frank and for his son, Lionel – it was not a
man's job to look after all the tiresome details of housework – and
sometimes she would even commiserate, with more of her heavy
underlinings, with their plight. How *awful* for the two of them to
have to live amidst such disorder and squalor! It was such a bad
example for poor Lionel, who had his career ahead of him and might
soon be setting up in a household of his own (my mother was in no
hurry at all to see *that* particular project realized). She also showed
some indulgence towards Miss Everitt; though she had never been up
in the enclave on the first floor, she had been able to remark on the
tidiness of her appearance, which, she suggested, was a sure
indication of good *breeding*. But this relative indulgence was
designed, whether deliberately, or, more likely, unconsciously – the
effect was the same – to weight the scales the more heavily against the
one remaining resident. Was she not in charge of the house? Did she
have no *pride* in its upkeep? She was not prepared to make any
allowances for the fact that Mrs Papé had to help out with the family
finances by teaching at Newlands two days a week; and there was
certainly no hint of solidarity as between two women who, at
different stages of their careers, had made a living by teaching art and

drawing in a school. When I had first been up to Percy House, I had thought that this might have counted in favour of Lionel's mother. But I was quite wrong. We had one or two of Mrs Papé's small water-colours at home. I thought them very pretty, I was particularly impressed by her ability to bring out the effects of bright sunlight on the white walls of a Welsh cottage. But my mother would defer judgment in such artistic matters, while going on to hint that Lionel, as an only child, had been dreadfully *spoiled* by his mother, who had molly-coddled him, had fussed over his food; one could see that at once. *She* could, anyway. I suppose, in my mother's view, no one would have been good enough for my sister, Diana.

I would listen to these much-repeated litanies and let them flow past me, as, a few years earlier, I had done the cross-examinations as to whether or not I had brushed my teeth before going to bed. No doubt, in previous years, my father, subjected to similar litanies, had been equally adept at appearing to listen, and even energetically to agree with the general drift of her criticisms, while mentally cutting off. He had also always given Lionel the warmest welcome. But he had died in the spring of 1935, so that I remained the only suitable witness to whom she could readily appeal. I felt that she would have liked me to share her disapproval, but that she knew that she would not succeed in getting me to do so. But, initially at least, her criticisms, her insistent questioning, especially about the quality of the food and the manner in which it was *served* — more rather ominous underlinings here — commenting, as if there had been no direct connection between the two sets of observations — that she did not think that Lionel had been looking very *well* in recent weeks, his colour had seemed to have been rather *poor*, and I suppose that she had the *plates* mainly in mind — must have made things very difficult for my sister.

I think Diana and Lionel had been informally engaged in my father's lifetime. Certainly Lionel seemed to have been around for a number of years, from when I was fourteen or fifteen. But they did not get married till 1937, by when Lionel had secured a job with a firm of chartered accountants in Chatham (a wise move, I thought at the time, placing the young couple at a fairly safe distance from my mother's insistent sollicitude). From then on, both my sister and myself got into the habit of referring to Frank and his wife, in very affectionate terms, as 'Father-in-law' and 'Mother-in-law', though it was impossible to include under such a heading Miss Everitt, for whom we had an equal affection. Lionel and my sister had originally met playing tennis at the Nevile Club; and, later, they had become the South of England champions in Mixed Doubles. Much that my mother had been gratified by the young couple's ability to shine at tennis – a game that stood high in her esteem (there had been a tennis court at Parkham, her father's house in Binfield and younger members of the clergy had been invited to the parties there in the 1890s), but, as I have suggested, she had certainly not initially approved of my sister's proposed partner in life as well as in Mixed Doubles, though mostly for rather *negative* reasons. The Papés were not included in my mother's regular Bridge-playing set: that was very much a point against them. Then, Lionel had not gone to a public school, or, rather, even *worse*, he had gone for a couple of terms to St Paul's, as a day-boy, and had then been withdrawn, or had withdrawn himself – the daily journey from Tunbridge Wells to Hammersmith and back must have been utterly exhausting for a teenage boy – opting instead for the local grammar school, Skinner's – a sensible enough decision, as it was just down the road from Percy House.

My mother did not see it that way. No, she would hasten to add, she had nothing against Lionel, it was just that he had never been given a proper chance. There had been, for instance, the manner in which he had apparently been brought up, or hadn't been brought up (my mother was always best on the sins of omission, Skinners', for example, was *not* a public school): first of all, being dragged constantly across Europe. She had nothing against Europe as such; but one had to fix on some single part of it, and not wander across the face of half-a-dozen countries. This had been no way to bring up a boy of school age (my mother's self-censorship had managed to eliminate Lionel's seven – no doubt unhappy – years at Newlands). Then there had followed a sort of *caravan* (it was wonderful what she could get into the pronunciation of that exotic word) existence in a whole series of houses. What about our *own* twenty-two moves within Frinton, or nineteen moves within Tunbridge Wells? She would sidestep that one by implying that it was not the number of moves that she was criticizing, but the *size* of the houses that they had taken on. They had all been much too large for them to have been easy to manage. They could easily have gone for something much smaller.

Once her four grandchildren, all boys, two of them twins, had been born, in less than four years, three of them war ones, my mother came to accept the situation, even developing a grudging approval of her son-in-law, who was visibly capable of 'managing', whatever she may have meant by that: again, I believe, another negative assessment, meaning that he did not live or behave like an artist (nor did his eminently middle-class parents and their friend, Miss Everitt; my mother was unaware of the fact that the decision to article Lionel to a chartered accountant, had been taken by his father, without consulting Lionel) and was at once proving adept at 'making two ends meet'. She always attached a great deal of importance to 'making two ends meet'. I suppose she had had to do, both as the seventh child of a country doctor who had lived in a very grand style, and throughout most of her married life. Lionel had passed, and passed with flying colours, this all-important test. Before very long, she even began to sing his praises and to quote him as an example to myself. She was delighted when he found himself a Reserved Occupation in 1940, a very shrewd move to have made in that alarming year. (My mother, though a terrible snob, had very little regard for the Services, though it would have been alright to have been a Surgeon-Commander, a position occupied by one of her brothers-in-law, or a Captain in the RAMC, one reached in wartime by her younger brother; I don't think her awareness ever extended to the RAF). Still, as I have said, she never made a second trip to Percy House; and when my sister and my brother-in-law came over from Chatham, or, later, from Hemingford Abbots, Lionel would always stay at his parents', my sister would come to stay with my mother's, and the babies would be distributed evenly between the two. I don't know how the arrangement had originally come into being, I never heard it discussed or questioned. In family matters of this kind, it is generally just as well to leave things unsaid.

I think Lionel always regarded Miss Everitt as a sort of honorary aunt; recently, he described her to me as someone who had been 'a mother to me', especially during his own mother's regular absences away in Seaford. It would have been hard to imagine Percy House without her, unobtrusive though her presence had no doubt always been. There would be little point in speculating on the economic circumstances that may have originally motivated, partly at least, a co-residence that had proved so enduring. It is possible that she may have contributed her share towards the actual purchase of the house in the early thirties. But there would be something rather indecent and clumsy in thus attempting to pry behind the deliberately uninformative screen provided both by the function – if there is one – and the rather uncertain title of being a 'companion'. I am quite certain that the word itself was never mentioned, at least in my hearing. It would have been most surprising if it had been. People who had long lived together and grown completely used to one another's company, adjusting easily to individual quirks and foibles, would not have seen the necessity of defining a relationship that had stood the test of time. Why indeed bother to define a function that was both happily vague and generally acceptable to all concerned? It was certainly one that seemed to have left Miss Everitt herself in quiet contentment, and that had always been taken as a matter of course by the other two, as well as by their son. 'Companion' was not some sort of badge to be worn in the lapel for the purpose of ready identification. One simply has to accept that the role of 'companion', however ambivalent, seems to have been a feature of middle-class domestic life readily accepted in Edwardian times and that had sometimes survived, as a relic of a more generous age, into the post-war period.

I was never very much bothered by such speculation from the moment, in 1936 or so, when I had first met the three of them. Miss Everitt had been there at my very first meeting with them; and the mere fact of her small presence had been a sufficient explanation. One easily accepts what might, with habit and further observation, have seemed the incongruity of a domestic arrangement by the simple fact of having been confronted with it for the first time; and I was not then in the habit of submitting every social situation, when faced with it, to what might have passed as a convincing historical interpretation, a form of *déformation professionnelle* that, applied to my perception of the attitudes of other people, came increasingly to dominate me later in life; and, in my very lack of curiosity, I may have been much nearer the mark than I am now. Could it not just have been that all four got on well together and that they had become dependent on one another's company? Certainly, by the time that I came to know them, the three elder residents seemed to have lost any inclination to look outside, beyond the strict limits of the chess club – a professional need, rather than a form of sociability, and one that his father had early on managed to communicate to Lionel, quite a figure in junior chess – the Nevile Tennis Club, or the preparatory school at Seaford.

I also think that Lionel's father may have been grateful for the unassertive presence at the dining-room table – the central forum of discussion between the long, arduous working hours upstairs – of the small, slightly bent figure in autumnal browns, as enabling him not to have been left in constant *tête à tête* with his wife, with whom he took a rather perverse and pucking delight in disagreeing, at least in the presence of outside witnesses such as myself – alone together, they may have got on perfectly well, or, equally, they may have found little to say to each other – about most of the public issues of the day; and, once the war had started, there would have been more and more subjects of apparently violent differences of opinion between the two of them. Mrs Papé revered Winston Churchill, so Frank would go out of his way to denigrate our wartime leader – I think, in this case, it was not just a matter of enjoying an argument for arguments's sake, but that his dislike of the ebullient and posturing politician may have been deep-rooted and may have dated from his own experience of war in 'the soft underbelly' area of the enemy powers, on the Greco-Bulgarian front. Or, on the contrary, he would sing the praises of our ally, Stalin, reminding his wife, in the later stages of the conflict, that the Red Army seemed to be in the process of winning the war for us. For he did not just have a rather Germanic – it may have been Scottish, too, the national origin of his mother – *penchant* for the cut-and-thrust of argument in the abstract, he was also something of a tease, as you could see from the sudden brightening of his eyes when about to come out with something calculatedly provocative. Religion, too, was a favourite stalking-horse of his. The teasing was mostly playful and good-humoured, designed to get a rise out of his rather literal-minded partner, who seldom failed him in this. I felt that, for the purpose of a game that seemed to have been recognized as such by both the active and the more passive participants, the quiet presence of Miss Everitt may have supplied the role of a sort of unofficial umpire, mutually recognized and generally silent, whose function was to ensure that the unstated rules of these round-the-table debates were respected. I never knew her intervene in these brisk exchanges of verbal tennis, all the best shots of which came from the aggressive male – at an earlier stage, so I had been told by his son, himself an absolutely first-class exponent of the real thing on grass – his less enthusiastic, much less nimble opponent contenting herself with rather feeble lobs, apparently mostly designed to keep the ball in play.

There was certainly no acrimony in these tea-time exchanges; and Mrs Papé seemed to have been as much an accomplice as an apparent opponent. Her complicity took the form of humouring Frank in the pursuit of one of his favourite public perfomances. Occasionally, Miss Everitt would permit herself a slight, timid smile at some particularly outrageous sally, as often enough on the subject of the Church Established. But this would be as far as she would allow herself to go. Mrs Papé was not his only sparring partner in these rather one-sided public debates. Much later in life, in his nineties, he was to take a malicious, gleeful pleasure in making gentle fun of my sister's attachment to the more social forms of religious observance. Did she then actually *believe* in God, in a Supreme Being? For the previous ten years, my sister had had to replace, however unsatisfactorily, his old partner in these games, who, like the umpire, had died in her eighties. Even at ninety-three or ninety-four, his eyes, though now quite unseeing, would still brighten as he was about to bring out a provocative remark in the direction of his daughter-in-law. But it would take two to conduct such an exchange; and Diana, unlike his old partner, would simply fail to respond, would not oblige him by rising to the bait, contenting herself with smiling tolerantly.

I know much more about Frank Papé than I do about his wife and Miss Everitt. As they may be presumed to have been very much of the same age, as they had attended the Slade together, it would seem permissible to apply the early chronology of his own life to that of his two co-residents. Frank was born, I think in Hamburg, of a German father and a Scottish mother, in 1878, making him two years older than my mother, at a time when the German Empire was itself only eight years old. The circumstances of his parentage gave him from birth the immense advantage of a double nationality, British and German. Lionel has described his grandfather to me, at different times, as a skilled watchmaker or a minor official. His great-grandfather, the painter of waterfalls, had been an early member of the Berlin Academy of Arts. Shortly after Frank's birth, the family had moved from Hamburg to Berlin, or maybe, back to Berlin, where Frank had gone through the exacting educational curriculum of Wilhelminian Germany up to the level of a *matura* on the completion of his studies at a *gymnasium*. One could no doubt read too much into these mixed origins, probably much commoner in a passportless pre-1914 Europe than in the post-war period; but it would be tempting to attribute to them, at least in some measure, something of his later mistrust of simplistic national stereotypes and of the cruder forms of jingoism. He was born a European and he was to broaden into a doubter given to questioning every *idée reçue*, both by education and as a result of personal experience and inclination.

I suppose that he must have been completely bi-lingual from a very early age. Though later very critical of most aspects of Wilhelminian society, he retained throughout his life an admiration for what he regarded as the sterling qualities of the German educational system: rigorous, professional, technically advanced, highly competitive, rich in abstract thought and very efficient in every discipline, and which he was in the habit of comparing favourably with the slap-dash amateurism of what he had seen and heard of schooling, both public and private, in this country. Frank held in little esteem the importance of 'character-building' and was wont to comment that it would not teach you how to draw. But I soon gathered from what he told me that, once in his late teens, he had begun to find the prevailing arrogance and militarism of Wilhelminian Germany, in its heyday in the 1890s, increasingly stifling and antipathetic. I could well understand his disillusionment, for it was clear that he had always been an extreme individualist, at least in his attitude to the State – I soon came to recognize in him both a mentor and a kindred spirit – and a natural rebel; and the servile conformism of his German contemporaries must have driven him further into conscious revolt. It would have been hard to have imagined a more improbable subject of the Kaiser: a conclusion that he himself seems to have reached early on in adult life. He may have been helped in this by his natural reluctance to undergo a period of military service to which he would presumably have been subjected on completing his studies.

Anyhow, somewhere round the turn of the century – he would have been twenty-two in 1900 – he had decided to cut his official, if not his family, links with Germany, and come to England – I don't think he had ever been there before, even to stay as a child with his mother's people – settling from the start in London. The date at which he took this crucial decision is, I believe, of a more general significance than as an episode in the life of this eager young Scotto-German. Frank must have been just *one* of a small army of immigrants from the two Central Empires – more, presumably, would have come from Vienna, Prague, Pressburg, Agram, Cracow, Lemberg, and Budapest, than from Berlin, Hamburg and Frankfurt – though Frank was aiming much higher than most of these, content to aspire to senior-servant status: head-waiters, *maîtres-d'hôtel*, *sommeliers*, and uniformed flunkies standing outside revolving doors. He was part of a general movement from Austro-Hungary and from Germany to England. But, in fact, he was not part of an *army*, for, unlike most of his fellow-immigrants, he had travelled alone, and, again, unlike the others, he had the unique advantage of being already in possession of British citizenship.

I don't know whether his parents had provided him with the means of continuing his education in what was still Victorian London. I don't even know whether they were still alive at the time, for I never heard him refer to either of them in all the years I knew him. This did not necessarily imply indifference or hostility on his part; there was no particular reason why a man already in his fifties should have talked about his parents to a young man still in his twenties who might be presumed to have had little interest in such relatively remote family matters. All I was ever told about his family by Frank himself was that he had had an elder sister, Ella, of whom he had been very fond and who had stayed on, either in Germany or in Austria-Hungary, thoughout the war years, had married a Czech, called Krečmar and had set up house in Vienna, where she had died of the Spanish flu epidemic, her resistance weakened as a result of extreme privation, in 1919, before her brother had had an opportunity to renew contact with her. I think he learnt of her death from her husband, but I don't know whether, at some later date, he ever met him. In view of their frequent trips to Austria, it seems likely that they would have done, some time in the early twenties. His parents may have helped towards the move from Berlin to London, but I think that it is more likely that, once there, he had made his own way.

It must have been a hard time for him, though the Edwardian music-halls and the big chess-playing *brasseries* seem greatly to have enlivened whatever leisure remained to the young man in his twenties, after no doubt pretty arduous and discouraging days hawking his portfolio of drawings and jacket designs round the precincts of St Paul's, Fleet Street and Bloomsbury. When I first got to know him, he was in the habit of evoking this remarkably free period of his life with a great deal of slightly aggressive nostalgia, perhaps because he had then been unencumbered with family. Viewed from the security and the changeless routine of Percy House, he had perhaps endowed his early years in London with the memory of the constant excitement of discovery, as the huge city had gradually opened up to the sharp-eyed young man fresh from Berlin. He wanted me to know – and the message may also have been addressed obliquely at his wife and Miss Everitt, for he would look at them with a lively insistence when talking of these early days – that he had thrown himself with a great deal of gusto into all the choices of boisterous entertainment available in a town unashamedly devoted to every loud and garish form of Edwardian pleasure, though he would have been too observant not to have noticed the extreme poverty and the wretched living conditions, the ragged children outside the beer-houses and the gin palaces that were likewise revealed in the harsh glitter of the urban night.

The early record of published work points to a very difficult, unpropitious start. Between 1902 and 1904, at a time when he had presumably completed his studies at the Slade, the only thing that had come his way was a contract to design the covers of a quarterly called, not very invitingly – it was not the sort of thing one would rush out to buy – the *Public Works Magazine*. However uninspiring the order, it did at least have the bleak advantage of tiding him over the next two years. But from 1904, when the programme of Public Works finally ran out, to 1907, there is no record of any commissioned work at all, though it is possible that he may have eked out a meagre living by taking in private pupils for lessons in painting and drawing. What seems, in retrospect, to have represented the breakthrough in his professional career came in that year in the form of a contract to do a whole run of covers and inside illustrations for *Cassel's Magazine* over a period of two years. This also seems to have introduced him to a market that offered the immense advantage of continuity, enabling him to look ahead and to make plans for the immediate future. In the seven years before the outbreak of the First World War, he was doing regular work for the *Pall Mall Magazine* and the *Boys' Herald*, the latter giving him a foot up into the steady run of children's publications, one of his main stand-bys for the rest of his working life. From 1908, there was a steadily expanding market for his work and by then he had established regular contacts with several of the wide-circulation publishers: Dent, Macmillan, and, above all, Nelson (the Bodley Head and the Oxford University Press would come later), as well as with the more specialized Duckworth. Ten years after his arrival in England, at the age of thirty-two he had succeeded in making for himself a successful professional career on the apparently firm basis of patiently accumulated contracts from a range of publishers specializing in children's books, fairy stories, myths, biblical stories, popularized potted history, picture books and annual school prizes. By 1911, he had established for himself a national reputation, and, in the following year – as we have seen, what could be described as his golden year – he had become so much in demand that it had been all he could do to keep abreast of the orders as they poured in, particularly at the approach of the Christmas season. Certainly, the decision taken to move to England had paid off handsomely in professional terms. I think it had, too, in personal ones. Frank had found more satisfaction in being English than he had previously in being German. And his second identity had been reinforced and enriched by an extremely happy marriage which was also, from the start, a working partnership.

I have tried to sketch in some of the ups and downs of his career over a period of more than sixty working years in so far as they may have affected the every day life of my three newly-found friends up at the top end of the town (the column devoted to Frank and his wife in Peppin and Micklethwait, *Dictionary of British Book Illustrators: the 20th Century*, ends, I find most appropriately, with the words: 'They lived for many years in Tunbridge Wells, Kent'). It is only very recently, and with the precious help of my nephew, Barry Papé, fourteen years after the death of his grandfather, that I have succeeded in establishing what seems to be a comprehensive list of his published work. At the time, I was not at all concerned to undertake anything of the kind. I had only the sketchiest knowledge of what Frank and his wife were doing in the studio upstairs, and I have only once actually seen Frank at work, wearing the tennis eye-shade, and that was not in Percy House, but in Bedford. I could hardly fail to know about the *Plaindealer*, I saw bits of it every day in the little coloured room, and the section devoted to luscious-looking, scantily clothed females would accompany me down to the other end of the town, ending up in my bedroom; and I had heard many times of the villainous Bedeaux, the strange Cabell, and the enterprising Denis Wheatley. But that was about the sum of it. Frank was much more likely to talk about Beachcomber (of whom he was a great devotee), or about the American film-actor, Harry Langdon, whom he enormously admired, than about his professional work.

From the start, I had been drawn to Frank Papé for his engaging irony, his habit of questioning everything, his sense of mischief, his enjoyment in deflating pomposity, his suspicion of power and of those who exercised it. The thing was that, no doubt like most young men in their early twenties, in 1938, 1939, and 1940, I was desperately in need of *advice*. What was I to do about a war that seemed inevitable, and that did indeed come? This, too, is where

Frank came in so providentially. I was very frightened; fear had been my dominant feeling pretty well all the time from 1935 or so. I wanted reassurance. Frank, I thought, was the sort of person who would have been able to look at the public scene as it were from a distance, and with the benefit of past experience. After all, he had been that way before, and he had *survived*; there was a crumb of hope in that. Furthermore, he had never been an officer, something I was easily convinced I could never be. Frank, by the mere fact of his survival, provided the rather exiguous consolation of *continuity*. Percy House also offered the additional consolation of the American connection. 'Uncle Ray', if not still out of the war after December 1941, was at least a comfortable distance from it. My own American connection, so desperately sought, in 1938 and in 1939, in the novels of Sinclair Lewis, and in many applications, all them predictably unsuccessful, to obscure Mid-Western Universities – Mid-America could never have seemed so attractive as during those terrible years – did not come till very much later in life, when I was approaching seventy.

Frank I have described as a 'natural rebel and mentor', so like my uncles Vernon and Jack. It just so happened – as a fringe benefit from my sister's marriage – that Frank was there and available, at the upper end of the town, and that very soon I came to admire his judgment, especially at a time when, as the result of the war and the breach with France, I was just beginning to try my hand at writing short stories, in an effort to perpetuate my French experiences, and to prolong them into the early, anxious months of exile: another form of *fuite en arrière*. The short stories were pretty bad, lush, and overblown; but at least Frank was prepared to listen to them and to offer suggestions as to how they could be improved on. Still, writing gave me a purpose in life during that awful period of waiting; it seemed one way to keep the alarming present at least at arm's length. Indeed, I went on writing, both in English and in French, right through the war years; and some of my pieces were published. It was only after my return to Paris, in the autumn of 1946, that my dependence on Frank became less urgent, and that I abandoned for a great many years my literary ambitions. But every time I returned home, the pull of Percy House would remain as insistent as ever.

Now I was less in need of advice and more inclined to tell the three of them of my own experiences. I no longer lived in constant fear, and so was less in need of reassurance.

Frank's face – and he was a very handsome man, with well-formed features, a fine brow, and grey eyes that were both kindly and very sharp – radiated intelligence and a sort of amused tolerance, as if he had never ceased to be astonished at the endless spectacle of human folly. There was always a lurking smile around the corners of his mouth, and I used to think that his usual expression of mild amusement had more than a hint of Voltaire, but a Voltaire less astringent, more benevolent, than the original. Though in extreme old age, once he had reached his nineties, his face had begun to cave in and shrivel up, the eyes still retained all their alertness and bright sparkle, even if they were by now sightless. I delighted in his irreverence: something that he shared with my two medical uncles, my mother's brothers, the Cobbs not being strongly endowed with that desirable quality – as in the agreeable emphasis of his voice – he spoke with a carefully modulated, rather stately, deliberation – but, most of all, in the extraordinary wealth of his visual observation and memory and his ability to transmit it. He had *seen* so much from the far side of the great chasm of 1914, and he could bring back to vivid life a gawky, adolescent Charlie Chaplin – aged twelve or thirteen – still uncertain of his gestures, and a gangling, bulbous-nosed W. C. Fields, dressed up in a long white tunic as a waiter and doing tricks with trays carrying full glasses, open bottles and tureens of soup, without allowing any of them to spill. He had developed a very early enthusiasm for the cinema and had been a fervent devotee of Max Linder. He carried so lightly with him the differing experiences of several decades: the 1890s of a brash, heartless, ugly, but immensely confident expanding Berlin; the rumbustious 1900s of an equally self-confident, vulgar, loud-mouthed, and rather boyish London: boyish in the sense that grown men seemed to have retained, well on into their thirties or even into their forties, a sort of still surviving boyish innocence and sense of fun. It was still there in 1914, one can see it on the faces of all those young men in boaters, cloth caps, and of those not so young, in jauntily tilted bowlers, queueing up outside the recruiting offices in the last weeks of that dreadful summer. But they seem to have been wiped off the faces by 1916. The Age of Innocence was over by then. Frank would also dwell nostalgically on the glories of a still amateur Wimbledon, which, even in the thirties, he would attend for the whole week; it was his one luxury, apart from chess. All this is what drew me up to Percy House, as to a second, much richer, more personal university than the one I was still attending or had just left. Under Frank's guidance one could almost *touch* the past and feel it as a physical presence.

But I have never been able to admire him for what I suppose he would have most wanted to have been admired and remembered: as an artist and an illustrator. I could never bring myself to appreciate his very mannered, drooping and consciously decadent style of illustration, a style rich, to the point of indigestion, in complicated loops and arabesques and carefully drilled trailing fabrics that seemed to drape themselves quite deliberately over inviting trellises or the curling head-rests of oriental sofas. It seemed to be unnatural, artificial and conventionally exotic, a middle-class Swan & Edgar exoticism, a visual rendering of some Palm Court musical score such as *In a Persian Garden*. It was too contained, too imitative – sub-Beardsley would have described it not too unkindly – and it lacked any trace of spontaneity. Even the elaborate signature, ending in a bold acute accent, and always enclosed in a decorative little box, seemed rather precious. It was a style that somehow *tried* too hard. One was insistently reminded of all the work and effort that had gone into it, under the white glare of the acetylene pressure lamp, almost as if the aid of rulers had been summoned. Indeed, I much preferred the pretty little water-colour sketches painted by his wife, or the delicate miniature pieces that reflected the neat personality of 'E', as she was known to Mrs Papé, little Miss Everitt. I even felt more at home with the unassuming and workmanlike line drawings poured out week by week for Uncle Ray. At least they represented recognizable historical figures, in correct period costume – Frank was a great stickler for getting the costume exactly right, down to the smallest detail: the buckles on the sandals of a centurion, the silken hose of a fifteenth-century knight – I would sometimes be consulted on the walking-out apparel of the transvestite Joan of Arc – though they were always well-covered, displaying not the slightest hint of bare arms and legs, even the Disciples went around in outfits that would have satisfied the demands of an Ayatollah, and Uncle Ray's little readers were well protected against anything the slightest bit unseemly, though I don't think Frank ever consciously catered for the prudery of a Mid-Western readership. These well-clothed historical characters appeared to be in normal health and were not afflicted, like so many of his vaporous mythical personages, with goitres, extended necks, or attacks of the droops.

His only interest to me as an artist was a purely historical one. His work seemed to epitomize, even to the point of caricature, an identifiable period of artistic vogue, something that would otherwise have been lost without a trace – no great disaster – but that, in this particular case, had miraculously survived well beyond its assigned decade, and had just gone on reproducing itself. 1914 had been the great divide in Frank's life, as in those of millions of others. But the hiatus would not have been in the least apparent in the style of his illustrations. Those of the twenties looked exactly like those of the 1910s. Something had got stuck somewhere, and that had happened at an early stage. Frank who, though he hardly ever read a newspaper (and that only for Beachcomber) and seldom listened to the wireless, was always so well up with current events, and who was anything but a stick-in-the mud, being well able to adjust to the changed circumstances of the twenties, the thirties, the forties and the fifties – and later still the poor man would have to try and cope with those of the sixties – appeared not to have budged an inch in terms of artistic style since his student days at the Slade and his successes of 1911 and 1912.

But there is no doubt that his work – whether in affectedly sinuous line, or in pen-and-wash had corresponded very closely to the prevailing tastes of the Edwardian market for fanciful and lavish book illustrations, flowery frontispieces, printed texts with twirling surrounds, and embossed golden filigree covers. Whether by luck or by calculation, he had been well married to his times as an emerging book-illustrator. By the age of thirty-three, in 1911, he had acquired a leading reputation in what must already have been a highly competitive field, at a time when the demands for picture books and copiously illustrated texts, including Bibles, seems to have been almost limitless. He could not have been better matched to the needs of a superbly confident and complacent middle-class and upper-middle-class reading public that craved for loops and twirls, droops and coils, not only in their books, but in their trailing, wide-sleeved summer dresses, in their curtains, in their upholstery. Indeed Frank might well have expanded into wallpaper and into furniture design, the latter in response to an equally insistent craving for wicker: baskets, work-baskets, chairs, garden-seats, even beds. One feels that he could have fully satisfied even the most minute demands of Mr Britling, his wife, and his large household when they had been in the process of setting up their well-stocked, extensive North Essex establishment in the spring and summer of 1914, for Mr and Mrs Britling's tastes seem to have been very exactly those of Frank. He could be most fortunate in his sense of timing; on the other hand, timing, as we shall see, could play him tricks that were both cruel and supremely ironical.

Anyhow, he had felt sufficiently assured of continuing success to have got married three or four years previously, 1907 (two years before that in which the other Frank had come over from Port Sudan or Khartoum to marry my mother); it must have been about then, for Lionel had been a child of six when, in early September 1914, on arrival with his parents (and Miss Everitt?) from a holiday in Switzerland at an embattled and chaotic Gare de Lyon – nearly seventy years later he could still recall the masses of men, sweating in their tight blue tunics and red trousers, their rifles piled *en faisceaux* – he had heard the not so distant continuous roar of what he was later – much later – to identify as the Battle of the Marne, then in full cry. The three of them were henceforward to live in the considerable style that I have described with reference to the large house taken in Surbiton, on the eve of the First World War – there had been two or three other large houses in the suburbs of South London before that – and with at least a couple of living-in servants. And Frank's optimism had, *dans l'immédiat*, been fully justified, orders coming in, as we have seen, with increasing regularity from half-a-dozen different publishers in the course of the next three or four years.

The Christmas season of 1913 had seen an unprecedented boom in huge Fairy Books of different colours, in boys' and girls' bumper annuals, in travel books: *Highways and Byways in Sussex, A Wan-*

derer in Paris, On Foot through the Holy Land – this was the high period of the stout-shoed walking tourist – illustrated in water-colours in muted shades, and school stories telling of last-minute edge-of-cliff rescues, or encounters with angry bulls, in flat, bold, plain colours, the schoolboy or schoolgirl faces exposed to the east wind off the German Sea or the South Wind off the English Channel, a uniform bright pink, the colour of ham.

At the time of the outbreak of the First World War, at the age of thirty-six, Frank had been at the height of his career as a much sought-after book-illustrator, many-hued armies of Fairies, Pixies, Gnomes, Witches, Devils, Woodland Spirits, Aladdins, Genii, Cinderellas, Sleeping Beauties, Captive Princesses with long golden hair drooping from high towers, Prince Charmings, ill-tempered, gruff-voiced Giants, Marchland Spirits and Manor-house ghosts now insistently claiming his services along with the Psalms of David, a very big order indeed. The seasonal demand had even spread to most *un*seasonal localities overseas: India, Ceylon, Burma, South Africa, Nigeria, Australia, New Zealand, perhaps as a nostalgic reminder of what Christmas would be like Back in the Old Country, but *not* the Sudan (its dreadful climate being rightly considered as unsuitable for European children). More suitably, perhaps, there was now an expanding market for the English Fairy Book among the upper ranks of an emerging and prosperous middle-class in St Petersburg and Moscow, Riga, Tallin, Odessa and Yalta, perhaps even Kiev. English pixies were beginning to come into their own in the wake of Scottish and English nannies and governesses, excellent apostles for Frank's line of business, and for the products of Dent, Blackie, Macmillan, and Nelson. Even after the outbreak of hostilities with the Central Powers, as the war was certain to be over by Christmas, it must have seemed that 1914 – a poor year, however, for Frank, with the lone *Indian Story Book* – would be just as good as the two previous years. With the war over in a matter of weeks, and a speedy victory secured, it might even be *better*, there would be even more to celebrate than usual. There would probably be a sharp decline in German fairies, giants and malevolent goblins, the Brothers Grimm were bound to be in less demand, but the gap thus left could be readily filled by the home-grown breed. In any case, Frank, possibly on ideological grounds – he had experienced German products from rather too close and seems always to have been quite anxious to separate himself from anything that might remind of what had presumably not have been a very happy Berlin childhood and adolescence – had never *done* the Grimms; and the stark cruelty of their stories would not have come easily to his mannered style.

But, as we know, and as poor Frank did not, matters did not work out at all like that. Christmas 1914 seems to have been moderately disappointing, with so many fathers not yet back home to light the candles of the bright festive tree (its German origins long since conveniently buried). Those of 1915 and 1916 must have been pretty grim for anyone involved in the book trade, though there would have been promising new openings, in the dailies, the weeklies, and the quarterlies, in the developing industry of anti-German pictorial propaganda of the Bernard Partridge School and even worse. Frank, needless to say, did not lend his hand to depicting the bestial features of the Hun and of the female of the species. It would indeed have been surprising, to say the least, if he had been tempted to portray, especially in crude caricature, the other half of his own identity; I imagine that he must have been sickened by the constant regurgitation of flat-topped heads, closed-cropped hair like piggy bristles, thick necks and slobbering lips. This I can only surmise, for I never heard him refer to a debased form of the art of illustration that seems even to have enjoyed quite a vigorous *post*-war respite, for by the time I joined the ranks of the reading public, in the early twenties, books for schoolboys were still liberally sprinkled with illustrations of Huns, both villainous-looking and plainly cretinous, being outwitted by Baby-Face Carruthers.

It was a very bad time then for Frank in particular: just one book, ironically, that of Russian stories, published in 1916, for the rest of the war years and the first two years of peace, till, in 1920, the providential arrival of Cabell on the scene. By 1916, too, many of those middle-class boys who had still been reading Fairy Books in the warm and comfortable security of spacious nurseries up on third or fourth floors, coal-fires blazing merrily in grates protected by high fireguards in 1910 or 1911, had already been killed on the Western Front. 1917 was to be even worse, as it reached out to clutch those male children who had formed perhaps as much as half of the bumper annual, school story and fairy book catchment area of the very end of the pre-war boom. It was such a quick, easy transition from reading about Little Red Ridinghood – or being read to about Little Red Ridinghood – to death as a second-lieutenant. 1917 also put a decisive end to the Russian market, there would be no looking back there, no return to normal, as, in that terrible year, and the two subsequent ones, children of middle-class origin – their appearance, their bearing, their good manners, their well-formed features, their good looks, their shyness, their cleanliness, their fine quality clothes, their educated speech would tell against them, would give them away to the watchful, observant rancour of class hatred – were systematically exterminated as such, along with their parents – Bulgakov, in his masterpiece, *The White Guard*, does, however, offer us some residual hope for the survival of at least a few members of a middle-class family, in the conditions prevailing in Kiev in 1918 and 1919, and in his novel there is even one character who dreams that no Revolution has taken place – though many of the British nannies and governesses who had read to them, did, happily, manage to get back home. By 1918, the old confidence had completely gone, though fairies and goblins did just manage to survive, but often under new management.

I don't know at what precise date Frank had volunteered for the army, nor whether he had chosen the Royal Army Service Corps or had simply been put in it. To one like myself who had only known him when he had already been in his late fifties, the decision itself would have seemed quite out of character. His evolution in the direction of a teasing and mischievous cynicism devoted to questioning every public attitude, may well have derived from the consequences to himself of what had been the result of a sudden patriotic impulse. By the time I came to know and to appreciate him, he would have been the very last person ever to have owned up to the slightest twinge of patriotism, even at some remote time in the past. But he had a way of censoring himself, if only to improve on the story; and whatever had originally motivated his decision to join up had been erased from such of the public record as was likely to be revealed to me, between puffs at his pipe and fumbling with its bowl, over the dining-table. Certainly, in 1938 and in 1939, his advice to me had been to keep out of any of the Services. Look what happened to *me*, he seemed to be implying, going on to tell me about his silly officers who had insisted, in what was a very quiet sector, in ordering their men to fire on the Bulgarian positions on the far side of a Greek river, only to provoke the peace-loving Bulgars into sporadic artillery activity. What nonsense it had all been, when both the opposing sides were only concerned with having a quiet time! I don't think he would have been at all perturbed – his wife would have been shocked to the core, and that, as so often, might have governed his own contrary attitude – if I had told him that I had decided to register as a conscientious objector, on religious grounds. He would have been tickled by that. He was always prepared to laugh at himself, as much as to say what a silly ass he had been and how he had been properly *had* (these would have been his very words, for he had retained well into the 1940s the music-hall boyish raciness of Edwardian popular speech.)

But, as far as I could make out, from a few chance remarks, and from what Lionel told me much later on, he must have joined up at the latest in the early months of 1915, that is at a time when the likelihood of the war being a short one had become very remote. First he had seen to it that the family would be provided for: his wife and Miss Everitt would stay at Newlands, the former as a member of the teaching staff (I don't think there can have been room for more than *one* art mistress) and Lionel would attend the school as a boarder. Although on the coast, Seaford seems to have been considered safe enough (so was my birthplace, Frinton, though, as it turned out, it was a good deal less so.) So with the family placed, he was left free to make his own way. He may of course have been influenced by the example of some of his male companions at the Slade; many of them would probably have opted for the Artists' Rifles, formed in the heady days of August 1914, and I suppose the name of the regiment might have drawn him too (not that he had ever had much time for artists as such). Anyhow, he had ended up in the much less prestigious Service Corps, which, apart from its many functions involving transport and supply, seems to have been responsible for camouflage. One should not under-estimate the compelling role of former *chums*, especially to a man in his mid thirties who, fifteen or sixteen years previously, had deliberately chosen the country of his mother's origins. It was clear, from many of his spicier reminiscences, that he had not always been a loner and had not always cut down his social contacts to a few members of the local chess club. Chums were still very much a social reality in the first two decades of the present century.

Having at least survived the war – and he would make much of this – at forty he had had to start again from scratch, and had in the end, as we have seen, managed quite well. He was still turning out his weekly series for Uncle Ray, though no longer from a frigid upstairs room in Percy House – his studio-cum-bedroom was now on the ground-floor of his son's big house in Bedford – till well on into his early eighties, when failing sight finally obliged him to give up, even the use of a jeweller's microscope attached over his remaining good eye now proving inadequate. Whatever one might say about his qualities as an artist, his professional career had been quite remarkably long, *too* long perhaps (he would have said so), as he toiled on alone for a further ten or a dozen years. As he so often complained, especially in the last years of his exceptionally long life, he had so often been a victim of timing, or that is how he would have seen himself, for timing had also sometimes been very kind to him, especially in the five years preceding the crisis of 1914. For instance, there had been a sudden up-turn in his prospects, in the second half of the 1930s, as a result of a brief nostalgic return to fashion of the mannered style of his generation of art students. It had even resulted in the possibility of a renewed contract with the Bodley Head; there had also been new work with Hutchinson's, a series of educational picture books, and the story of the Crown Jewels, the text of which was provided by his wife. By the time I first came on the scene, quite a lot must have been going on upstairs. But 1939 had dried up the market, leaving Uncle Ray and the prep school as the sole providers. Then, much later, just as his sight was completely failing and he had at last to give up, there had come a second, previously much-longed-for call from the Bodley Head, as well as one from the Oxford University Press, who had expressed a renewal of interest in projects that had been mooted and then dropped many years before:

pictorial histories – the Romans, the Anglo-Saxons, the Normans, and that sort of thing, for children, and perhaps illustrations for another Book of Psalms. 'Just my luck, Richard', he would say, wrily, 'something I had been hoping for for years, and they have to come up with it just when I am more or less blind!'

It was as if his artistic career had been plagued by a recurrent time-pattern, subjecting him (with his Continental turn of mind, he might have appreciated that, as a wry testimony to his 'otherness') to the iron demands of some mysterious historical law. His own version would have been that he had reached the top of his form and his popularity in 1914 – this had not been quite the case, his best year having been 1912 – when the coming of the First World War had brought a sudden end to a professional career now reduced to the derisive consolation of camouflage work for the RASC. The first flickers of an unexpected revival of interest in his line of work had been at once extinguished by the outbreak of the Second World War: again he had fiddled a bit with the chronology, the 1930s having been relatively prosperous. No wonder he had come to see himself as the chosen victim of outside events, of Warring Powers. There had been a good deal of reason in his deep-rooted and impassioned individualism. And, on this subject of timing, he would certainly have been tickled by the thought that, more than fourteen years after his death, several rather obscure enthusiasts, teaching in North Country Polytechnics or Municipal Art Schools, in places that he had never visited and had barely heard of, should have set out, unbeknown to one another, on exploratory journeys to Tunbridge Wells, in search of the former pupil of the Slade and the owner – or part-owner – of Percy House. I could almost hear his emphatic laugh: 'Richard, a lot of good THAT would do me!' His priorities had been much more modest: not fame, not even a grudged recognition, certainly not the admiration of some unknown enthusiast, but just to be paid for the work that he had already done.

It is time to take leave both of Percy House and of its three inhabitants, though the partings were not to take place exactly at the same time. The house in fact did not follow the example of the conservatory, and fall down about their ears. Early in the 1960s, Frank, his wife and Miss Everitt had all reached their eighties, I think more or less together; and the house, in whatever state of advanced dilapidation it had now reached, was beginning to prove too much for their failing physical powers. Frank had put the house on the market, and the three, including the entire contents of their separate studios and all the furniture – even that of the former drawing-room; only my beloved stained-glass had been left behind – had moved to Lionel's and my sister's large house up the Kimbolton Road in Bedford (appropriately, the house is now an old peoples' home). Within six months of their moving in, Mrs Papé and Miss Everitt had both died, I think in that order, Miss Everitt would never have asserted herself by pushing to the front, especially on such an important occasion: companions still, as they had been for sixty years in life. But Frank lived on for another dozen years or more, dying in May 1972, at the age of ninety-four. By then, he was completely blind, could only move with difficulty, almost doubled up, with the help of a frame, and only occasionally emerged from the ground-floor flat that had been carved out of the house for him and where he was looked after, during the last weeks of his life, by a full- time male nurse. I saw him a few weeks before his death. The voice was as strong and as agreeable as ever, as he playfully ribbed my sister about her activities with church bazaars and similar worthy causes. But when he heard my voice, he turned his blind face, still handsome, in my direction, saying, with careful emphasis, as if he had been dictating, and utter conviction: 'Richard, I am so bored'. He had lived very fully, but too long. Even so, I was glad to notice that he was still wearing his old familiar oatmeal-coloured suit, now hanging off him.

Percy House had been sold, for a disappointing price, to a local Tunbridge Wells building contractor. Rather than attempt to carry out repairs, the purchaser had had the house demolished – I think he had used his own bull-dozer – and had sold the land, at considerable profit, to a garage firm. In its place, there is now a big, garish petrol station and a large motor showroom. Frank had never been told of what had happened to his house; and his son had managed to prevent him from making a special trip to Tunbridge Wells to see for himself (and look up some of the chess club people). Percy House had suffered the same fate as St Leonard's House in the Hythe. Petrol stations don't give much away.

SIX

Both Sides of the Tracks

Columbia, South Carolina, May 1987

'I ALWAYS see you here on Sundays', I said to the Indian lady, as she was rubbing down one of her two big black dogs with a vast white bath towel, while the other one, with a yellow tennis ball in his mouth, shook himself on the grass, scattering drops over my thin summer trousers. I had seen her at exactly the same spot, sitting on the same green bench, on the Horseshoe, on a succession of Sundays that stretched from January to May. As this was my last Sunday, I had decided to speak to her. I had thought that she would be there – I always came through between 9.30 and 10 – and she was, and this pleased me. 'Yes', she replied, 'it is something of a ritual, first they go for a swim in the pond, then they play ball, then I dry them with a towel'. It's a pity I won't see her again. Maybe *next* Sunday she'll be looking out for *me*?

Ritual, I thought, was exactly the right word for it, it was what it was all about. It was surprising really how quickly I had established my own, without any conscious effort at planning; it was just that I had soon found myself doing the same things and observing the same objects and the same people at the same times. It was something to hold on to and that gave a soon familiar structure to the day, the week and the month. *Ritual* was something that I had always carried with me, packed away in a suitcase, every time I went off to some unfamiliar place, so that it would be at once ready to hand and adjustable to local conditions. It was just like changing the time, or the voltage of an electric razor. It had worked here too, even better than usual, though it had taken a little time – a fortnight or so – fully to set it up.

155

It had started at the drugstore on the corner, with our first encounter with the barber, when he had heard our accents. 'Doctor', he had asked, 'are you from Oxford? Do you know Dr John Walsh?' I replied that we were and that we did. I did not tell him that I was *not* a Doctor, so a Doctor I remained for the next four months. In the copy of his book, *Southern Folklore*, that he gave me, he has written inside: 'To Dr Richard Cobb, "Leader in Education"', so maybe I am that, too. The 'Leader in Education' soon made a regular habit of getting his hair cut at the place at which he worked. At one time it had been his own shop, but, he told me quite cheerfully, he had been bought out or sold out, and he now worked there for someone else: a young man with a beard who, along with Mr Saylors, employed half-a-dozen female hairdressers in the two adjoining shops.

The barber was a lean, outdoor man in an indoor job, talkative, like all barbers, and accompanying his talk with a high giggle of a laugh 'Tee-Hee'. He wore a check shirt, and he had a creased face, the way some American faces crease and British ones don't. He looked about fifty to fifty-five, but was in fact seventy-four. At some stage of the war – 1944 or 1945 – while in the US Rangers, he had been caught behind the German lines and had been hidden for three days by a Dutch family, with whom he had kept up ever since. He talked too of lying very still in a foxhole, looking down the long vicious black muzzle of a Tiger-Tank ('Tee-Hee'). At the time of the dropping of the Atom Bomb he had been due to embark for the Japanese mainland on the *Queen Mary*, which had taken him to New York City instead: what a bit of luck! ('Tee-Hee'). He seemed to have been in the way of encountering celebrities. Indeed, some of these appeared to have made a point of seeking *him* out. He had saluted General Montgomery, who had then shaken his hand. He had cut the hair of President Nixon. He had *seen*, and talked to, President Roosevelt, and had cut the hair of his three bodyguards. President Kennedy had arrived with twelve bodyguards, and he had cut *their* hair. And, of course, he had also met Dr John Walsh, of Oxford.

He might have come off one of the covers of the old *Saturday Evening Post*, he had a weathered, *country* look about him, and his book was a description of his childhood in a very poor rural area of South Carolina. He had a wide circle of friends in the town. On my most recent visit, he had introduced me to one of them, as he was leaving the chair: 'Doctor, meet the Doctor, he's a medical Doctor, he can *kill* people' ('Tee-Hee'). Several of his friends were people whom he had trained as youngsters and who had set up in their own establishments. He claimed that South Carolina offered especially favourable conditions to barbers, it was something to do with the hot, humid climate which made both hair and nails (not his line of business, though he was very good on *eyebrows*, and had been told by John L. Lewis not to touch *his*, as well as on hair sprouting from the ears, a sure sign of ageing) grow at twice the speed they would have done in Maine or New Hampshire. He may have had something there, for *my* hair and nails had grown amazingly fast. But, despite these local advantages, his own career had been anything but a success story; but he did not seem to mind, indeed rejoicing in the affluence of some of his former pupils. He was a small-town character in a small town. Many of his customers went to him to listen to his talk and to his high-pitched laugh, as much as to get their hair cut. He was a very skilled barber and always put on his steel-frame spectacles when he had someone in the chair. He did a neat job for children, making them laugh while he worked on their fringes. He had a most soothing hand when he applied a hot towel to the back of one's neck or of one's head; he told me that he had perfected this particular technique on his wife, when she had been tired at the end of the day. If one returned to the town, the barber would be the first person one would look up. One would know where to find him; he would be in the shop, always at the far end, and would resume the chronicle at the point at which he had left off a year or two before ('Tee-Hee'). He was a reassuring sort of person.

There were other familiar sightings, especially a black man on crutches with his right leg amputated just below the knee. He could be spotted in any part of the town. He always seemed to be in a hurry and could cover a lot of ground at speed on his crutches. Perhaps he was one of *several* black men with their right legs amputated just below the knee, but I think he was just himself, not part of a team of town-crossing one-legged blacks. He was very shabby, with an old, soggy, long-peaked cap in a colour no longer definable, but with faint hints of red, and he looked as if he was very poor. There was always an urgency about his movements, but they did not seem to lead in any particular direction – I have seen him suddenly turn round and head off in the direction from which he had been coming; the way that he hobbled along at a spanking pace, with his loping gait, he might have been taking exercise, just to keep fit; but he did not *look* very fit. I must have spotted him, over the months, in a score of different locations.

Nearly all the big roadside signs had some of their rather shabby insertable yellow or red letters falling out, missing, or askew; some had jumped into the next line down, producing odd sorts of codes: *THRU-IN BREAKFAST WITH A WARM SMILE*, on the way from the airport, or down among the jungly, tatty, dusty no-manslands – not yet quite a city, but an indication that it is on the way, its long-drawn-out unlovely fringe, on and on for miles – of Rentacars, Mobile Homes, wooden houses on wheels awaiting removal, and little Drive-In banks with confusingly similar names, the wind raising up a swirl of empty packing-cases and discarded carrier-bags. At Billy Graham's Mission in the huge football stadium (to seat 75,000) the dirty yellow letters spelt out: *JESUS: I AM THE WAY AND THE LIFE* (the final E was leaning over to the right), they were on the enormous score-board, above *SCORE*, and *HOME* and *AWAY*, all of them lit up in a yellow electric glow: I suppose Jesus and his message could not be disconnected from the line below. I was struck by such a curious juxtaposition of the reverent, the commercial, and the sporting, the packaged warmth, the message wrapped up, no, not wrapped, just *put*, like a pack of *Bud*, into a brownpaper bag. The same insertable red or yellow letters might witness for a fast-food, or for a pre-cooked religion, a fast-salvation: *HARDEE, DELI, PIZZA HOUSE, CHINESE GARDEN, THE CHURCH OF GOD*, or *PIGGLY-WIGGLY'S*. They conveyed an odd sense of the inappropriate, perhaps a certain vulgarity, but also a refreshing lack of pomposity, even a rather engaging candour. The lines of little coloured nylon flags – red, a livid blue, pink, a hideously hygenic white, an emerald green, fluttering, not very invitingly, in the wind straight down from Canada, and hinting at a ghastly sort of jocularity, a tinfoil *fête* (like the birthday balloons brought in ceremoniously to a restaurant table, or placed on the outside balconies of houses, in mournful clusters) in front of tyre depots, second-hand car emporiums, Deposit Stores, and seedy-looking motels (but not outside Funeral Homes) – provided tawdry decorations that seemed to be putting out elequent signals of avoidance: 'Do not buy', 'Poor quality', 'Shoddy material', 'Pass on'. They reminded me too of the lush, over-luxuriant foliage of the shiny nylon flowers placed in clashingly-coloured profusion over recently-dug graves, the graves themselves covered by elaborate, shiny blue and red canopies on poles, taken down the same day, leaving the flowers sodden and forlorn, till their removal, no doubt for further use.

The flags, the lettered messages, and the garish nylon wreaths formed part of the habitual scene of going out and coming in, so I warmed to them, too. After all, they were no doubt well-meant, in their toothy commercial welcome; and there was something rather pathetic in the brave attempts of the pointed flags to give at least a veneer of desirability to objects most of which seemed irredeemably unlovable and easily disposable. I suppose one should always give a little credit to anything that tries so hard, and the little flags did at least lend a bit of colour, albeit artificially lustrous and endlessly washable, to a pretty hopeless landscape in which sombre greens, dusty greys, dull scrub, an anaemic beige, and squat, hasty buildings competed unhappily with the uniformly blue glare of an implacable sky.

But what gave the town its *uniqueness* – for the approaches to any American town are depressingly similar – and what provided it with a strict measure of time, was the *train*. The train also offered a wonderfully visual indication, if indeed one were needed, of the sheer *vastness* of the country, the majestic, slow-moving, hooting and ringing mile-long topography of a continent, as if the train had a secondary, didactic purpose to spell out, on the huge red, black, and yellow sides of the freight-cars and the car-carriers, and the big, jet-black locomotives, a selection of the points of the compass, with the emphasis on *SOUTH* and *SOUTHERN* – a rightful priority – but also on *EASTERN*, and, rather mysteriously, *WESTERN*, with only *NORTH* and *NORTHERN* missing (*NW* is not what it seems to be, the white letters, enlaced, on the black sides of the tall cars stand for *NORFOLK & WESTERN*), so an incomplete compass, with the most prestigious and the most alluring point left out (at least as such, for there is a very occasional sighting of *BOSTON & MAINE*). Perhaps the north is just too far away, even for this gigantic and oddly-assorted, mile-long train, fronted by a great clanging bell and three or four black locomotives, placed back to back, and terminated in a little, almost miniature, red guardsvan marked in white letters *SOUTHERN*, in a timid effort to affirm the last word, and, not forcefully, but humbly, to contradict the bold front *NORFOLK & WESTERN*, rather as if the west had been given the heavy job of pulling the south along behind it. Or so it seems, for *SOUTHERN* easily outnumbers all the other variations, as if these had been slipped in just to add a sense of novelty and change. The little guardsvan, a brighter red than the sister freight-cars, and half their height, has an oddly domestic appearance, with a tiny open platform carrying a bench at its very end, rather like the open balconies with their hammocks and their rocking-chairs, of the elaborate neo-classical wooden houses, their cushion-capped Doric and Ionic pillars hollow inside. The sense of domestic ease and intimacy is further accentuated by the long thin metal chimney projecting from the white roof of the van, indicating the comforting presence in the shadowy interior of a wood-burning stove.

So a big train for a big map. An outsize train for an outsize country. A long train as if to measure up the length of the mysterious journey from somewhere to somewhere, but always through the town, in order to assert some ancient right of passage. It is also a human train at the beginning and the end, with a couple of men in check shirts, their sleeves rolled up, and caps with long peaks, and with their feet up, in nonchalant ease, in the first of the three or four black locomotives, coupled together, and more men, dimly seen, sitting down on a bench inside the little red guardsvan. They rarely sit out on the open platform, looking backwards. Perhaps they have seen it all before, many times, having watched the shining rails twisting and turning and disappearing behind them, and have got *bored*, preferring to sit and smoke inside, or to play cards. Maybe all that they have to do is to see that the red tail light, the final message left by the train, has been turned on at the beginning of the journey, when the train had been formed up and given its varied composition and its assigned loads: chemicals one day, kaolin the next, coal and wood the one after, huge containers every day, cars, scrap-iron, metal shavings. But, one day, at my evening watch at 6.19, I struck lucky: this time, two men, in check shirts and wearing baseball hats, *were* out on the open platform, as if they were enjoying the view and the still fierce sunshine. Perhaps they were newcomers to the route. They grinned and waved to the small crowd that had formed up at the crossing on both sides of the train and that, in their wake, hastened to cross the tracks. The two men, one of them lean and leathery and with grey hair and steel spectacles, seemed to be enjoying themselves. They had the advantage of a commanding position, high up above the tracks, and one occupied, in the old days, by politicians and Presidential candidates on whistle-stop coast-to-coast tours. I stood watching them as they disappeared from view round a curve in the line: two men, in casual clothes, as they watched stretches of their immense country unwind, mile after mile, behind them. Or maybe it was the town and the onlookers that had brought them out. I have always thought that the view from the back was the best. No doubt they would have agreed.

The men in the front with their feet up always wave to passers-by, six feet below them; waiting at the crossings or on the grass verge of the sloping pathway, they raise a hand in greeting and grin, as the people down below wave to them; it is quite an easy-going communication, as the train makes its stately and majestic way through the centre of the town – it is very much part of the town – not hidden away in deep cuttings or in discreet tunnels; indeed, several times a day, and as many during the night, it *divides* the town, and the town has to wait for it before being reunited. At night, its hooting passage – like a huge, mechanical owl – causes the inhabitants of the town to stir in their sleep or turn sleepily towards their partners, like the 4 am carriages of the returning gamblers in Restif's Parisian nights, producing additions to the local population; it is a reassuring sound, indicating that all is as usual.

There are then the two reclining figures right up front and the two or three sitting inside the little red van, with no human presence in the mile or the mile and a half that separates the two groups, though there are plenty of empty freight-cars, their sliding doors wide open, to reveal traces of straw and dirty bits of packing cases, most of them marked *SOUTHERN*, as if they had already carried out their assigned tasks. The days of the hobo are over.

The train, on *good* days – on bad ones it will just be *SOUTHERN SERVES THE SOUTH*, to the right, and *SOUTHERN GIVES A GREEN LIGHT TO INNOVATIONS*, to the left, all the way (though the letters about the Green Light are often so dirty as to be barely visible) – is rich in romantic allusions: *RIO GRANDE, SANTA FÉ, THE COTTON BELT, NORTH FLORIDA & GULF, GEORGIA PACIFIC, UNION PACIFIC, FLORIDA & EASTERN SEABOARD, TRANSMERICA, ORIENT & OVERSEAS CONTAINER LINE (OOCL), EVERGREEN* (livid green containers), the prestigious *CP*, the *almost* as prestigious *CN* (*National* is always a bit of a let-down, especially when compared with *Pacific*), both of which have managed to stray down from Canada to the Deep South, the elegant *THE VIRGINIAN*, with its suggestion of literary associations (it is carrying to the brim a load of coal), the slightly sinister *ILLINOIS & TERMINAL*, the terse *READING*, and, in bizarre combinations, *MARIETTA, TOMAHAWK & WESTERN RAILWAY, BOSTON & MAINE, BURLINGTON & NORTHERN, LANCASTER & CHESTER* (not so ill-assorted after all), *GEORGIA CLINCH-BURG & WESTPOINT*, memorials perhaps to now extinct, or, at best, declining, railroad systems that linked improbable places, perpetuating their duos and their trinities in a still lingering popular memory. Then there is a hint of Southern ease and comfort about *SOUTHERN SUPER-CUSHION SERVICE*. Railroads are also Systems, doubling up as *THE DELAWARE & ORTEGO SYSTEM, THE SEABOARD SYSTEM* (it must surely be the *Atlantic* one?), but then, all at once, deftly slipped into the pack when no one was looking, like a trump card banged down in triumph, *THE MISSOURI & PACIFIC SYSTEM*, a very big order indeed, followed, lamely, by the enigmatic *THE CHESSIE SYSTEM*. Some straddle – or make that bold claim – the whole length and breadth of the enormous land mass: *THE NATIONWIDE BOXCAR POOL*, asserting, jauntily in red and blue letters, and snake-like fanged pointers: *NEXT LOAD, ANY ROAD,* on a dirty yellow background, in its own attempt at rhyme.

The Pool prepares the way for the surprise intruder, *THE MILWAUKEE ROAD*. What is a *road* doing somewhere down the middle of this apparently endless, rumbling, banging (the huge wheels of some of the big, dirty *SOUTHERN* freight cars need adjusting), screeching (they need oiling too as they protest angrily in fatigue), many-coloured, visual song of praise to a railroad topography that brings down to this southern level *NORTH DAKOTA, SOUTH DAKOTA,* and *NEBRASKA,* on the sides of trucks, but that insolently ignores New York and Chicago?

The train is the most eloquent emblem of the town that it so imperiously divides, making its inhabitants, in cars, on bicycles, on big Japanese motor-cycles, or on foot, await its sovereign pleasure, as it proceeds inexorably, and in studied slowness, and, tantalizingly, allowing the pedestrians holding big brownpaper bags (*FOODLION*) of food and drink in both hands, to glance through the spaces left by the empty container-carriers, and briefly to glimpse the far side and to get ready to cross over – 'this *must* be the end of the train' – before that impatient shore is once more blotted out, as if in mockery, as much as to say: 'You thought that was the *end* of me and that you could get across the tracks, but you were *wrong*, just wait and see, there is plenty more of me yet to come', repeating the trick with two or three more apparently promising gaps, before the appearance at last of the little red guardsvan (the *Kaboos*).

In the day, the train thus asserts its feudal rights over the town. It also plays other tricks, this time on the *ears* of the inhabitants, hooting and honking very loud, as if it were just about to appear round the corner, at the bend of the shining line, at the bottom of the footpath, then going quiet for ten minutes or a quarter of an hour, before emitting a shattering blast from an opposite direction, giving the impression that it had turned on its tail, and was approaching from the other side. This game of aural hide-and-seek might be kept up on and off through much of the day: a faint, distant, echoing hoot from the west, followed by an insistent honk from the east, then silence: 'I am coming, no, I am not', content apparently to lurk somewhere on the fringes of the place, just for the fun of it: an orchestration of sounds designed to assert its elusive presence or absence, like an invader tentatively probing the outer defences of the city, then hastily withdrawing, to take up new positions in the rear.

At night, it reigns alone and unobserved, save by some long-distance truck-driver as he waits by the crossing at Five Points, but vaguely heard and sensed, a bit blurred, like the peaks of a mountain-range emerging from the clouds that conceal the lower slopes, by the sleeping residents: a gentle presence, marking out the safe passage of the night hours, a changeless, discreet chronicle of reassurance. A totally silent night would be much more alarming, in the absence of the muffled hoots of the slow-moving train and the steady, distant, even rumble of its wheels. Perhaps its watchful, muted presence might penetrate dreams; certainly it would help children sleep in peace.

Of course, we had been told about the train before we came here, so that its single distant hoot, within an hour of our arrival, was instantly recognizable and seemed like a greeting of welcome to the three newcomers, admitting them to the warm intimacy of common experience, like a password to which we had been given the secret meaning, offering the comforting thought of familiarity with a town and a community to which we had come for the first time and in which we were complete strangers.

The keys to reassurance are familiarity, habit, a routine rigorously adhered to, but varied to suit the particular needs of each hour and each day, so as to give both a recognizable and distinctive identity: *Sunday* morning, to collect the *New York Times* at the newstand on the right of Main, opposite the State House; 6.19 *each evening*, by the sloping footpath, to see the train, then, once round the block, and two cats to stroke; *Saturday morning*, at 8.30, to Grice's (Fruit & Vegetables), then to Kroger's; a *Tuesday* lecture and class, a *Thursday* lecture and class; *Monday, Wednesday* and *Friday*, to pick up William from A. C. Moore's the school in Richland County, then a wave to the smiling black policewoman (a Jehovah's Witness) on the corner carrying her round STOP sign; Lunch *every day* save Saturday at Yesterdays, something of a misnomer, as it has soon established itself as today, tomorrow and the day after, tailing away into a predictable future. Familiar objects regularly noted, and familiar people encountered where one expects them to be can be recruited to the same purpose. All will contribute to a sense of continuity, even in a period as short as four months, for routine and habit are easily adjusted to the claims of an unfamiliar place and to a completely new time-table. Frank Norman has written that even prison can be reassuring, because it imposes an utterly immobile division of the hours, the days, and the nights, a distinctive week and a distinctive Sunday. In other words, it has succeeded in disciplining the future into *utter* predictability. No wonder many old lags contemplated with something like terror the prospect of being let out into a timeless limbo that lay beyond the gates.

Primus took some fifty years to tighten up, perfect, and, eventually, to immobilize, within a minutely regulated time-frame, *his* sense of continuity. The result was a small masterpiece, with every *minute* accounted for. But it was *too* perfect, and when he was turning seventy – an age when routine and habit become even more insistent – like an over-wound watch (and his whole-hunter was the regulator of his minutely organized life) it fell to pieces, and he was left completely at sea. It was too much for him to construct a new routine in an unfamiliar place, and emptiness and bewilderment filled his days, all his defences were washed away, and he went mad. (It was perhaps in character that one form taken by his madness was the belief that some of the elderly ladies who shared his boarding-house had designs not just on *him*, but also on his whole-hunter, which he took to hiding under his pillow at night). Yet, from twenty or so to seventy, he had acted with *wisdom*, leaving himself no possible exposure to the unpredictable, and keeping outside events at a safe distance. He had even managed to accommodate the dreadful Great War to his domestic needs; Paxman's was just over the garden wall, so that he had been able to retain his familiar base, he could have all his meals at home and could sleep every night in his own bed. Working during the day as an engineer in a war factory was a small price to pay for so much home security. To sleep in one's own bed is a minimal priority, enabling one to emerge from sleep and from the perils of the night to familiar sights and sounds. Of course, I never saw inside my uncle's bedroom; but I imagine it was cluttered with objects, all in their rigorously assigned places. What Primus had not calculated for – how *could* he have done, it was a prospect too awful to contemplate? – was that his parents would die in their nineties, leaving him an orphan at seventy.

Even Daisy, in her sloth, showed considerable elements of wisdom and self-knowledge. I don't know how old she had been when 'Charlie' and 'Mrs Ma' had died: probably in her middle or late sixties, giving her some forty years habituation to a life of drifting between sleep and dozing, of *Daily Mail* fantasies, hearty meals, and regular *sorties*, never very far afield, and exercising her talents on my grandmother's piano in the evening, before an early night – 'Early to bed, Late to rise' seems to have been her own highly successful slogan for her nights and her days. Unlike Primus, I don't think that she had ever made any conscious calculation, she had never been an organisation person. But there again for her continuity had been brutally snapped when the old man had died and when she had had to get out of her familiar bed and her familiar bedroom.

So, in their modest, totally unambitious way, both Primus and Daisy had illustrated a very basic wisdom that had measured up to their very limited expectancies. They had not asked for very much: just to be allowed to go on as before and to continue along the iron rails of accumulated habit. Their wisdom had taken differing forms: Primus had lived by his watch, Daisy had floated outside a fixed time-scale, though there had been a sort of untidy regularity about the late hour of her rising and her early hour of retiring to bed. She seems to have carried her personal clock inside her, dispensing her from the need of possessing a time-piece or of taking in the evidence displayed by the grandfather clock in the dining-room when it struck the hour (I assume that she could tell the time, but that it was too much of an effort for her to do so). The wisdom of Primus was that of the drill-sergeant, he was tidy to the point of fussiness, and always made his own bed; no doubt, it would have successfully stood up to the minute scrutiny of a kit inspection. Daisy's wisdom took a lethargic form: the negative art, carried to near-perfection, of doing nothing, or of doing as little as possible: a strict economy of action. For Daisy, *doing* was to encounter danger, and reassurance and security were to be found in inaction. Doing nothing carried its own built-in continuity. *Action* could be a hostage to the unexpected. Much of the continuity in Daisy's restricted, low-key version of life was assured above all by the long hours of *sleep*. Perhaps she slept the sleep of the just, perhaps she was never afflicted with nightmares; perhaps, unlike Ahab, she never turned her face to the wall, but slept, like a child, facing towards the window and the high-walled garden. It was a solution of a sort. Unlike that adopted, polished and perfected by Primus, it made no allowance either for tidiness or for punctuality. She *thrived* on slovenliness and disorder: better not to change the sheets but to sleep in soiled ones, for they had done service for weeks and months before; better not to throw anything out, for the accumulated *Daily Mails* – thousands of them, tens of thousands of them – supplied the *visible* evidence of continuity back in time, stretching back over the years, and if continuity ran *backwards*, it might be presumed to run *forwards* as well. (Perhaps I am crediting Daisy with too much perception, for I don't think that she ever did much *thinking*, but she may well have worked out something of the kind in her rather blurred way. Anyhow Teddy Tail was *timeless*, he lived outside time, there had never been a point at which he had been *born*, he had always been around, changeless and fully-grown, he always wore the same clothes and the same socks and buckle shoes, and he would never grow old, would never *die*, he was a rock in the stormy ocean: Daisy had chosen well.) Better not to change a dress when one had one that almost stood up on its own, so used had it become to its wearer's contours. Like Primus, Daisy was an enemy of change; but for *her*, change – radical and dangerous change – would take the form of soap and water. Dirt was the past, the present and the future, a bulwark of continuity. So continuity could best be assured in layer upon layer of bodily dirt. My mother's efforts to clear out Daisy's room and to clean up Daisy herself represented a brutal, if uncalculated, assault on Daisy's patiently accumulated defences. This was not something that my mother could have understood. There are many personal forms of continuity. My mother, over the years, had built hers on the firm foundation of tidiness, neatness and cleanliness, of polishing and sweeping, of ironing and folding, of 'putting things away in their right places'. Of course Daisy was able to reassert her own recipe for continuity, a single bath would only be a temporary breach in her massive fortifications of neglect, untidiness, and ancient dirt. It must have been a shock, but the sheets would soon resume their greyish colour, the papers would once more pile up on the unmade, crumpled bed and on the floor, *Teddy Tail* would be back in business, and Daisy would no doubt forget the horrifying experience of the scrubbing-brush, encased once more in the protective covering of ancient and recent dirt.

I have now reached the age at which Primus found himself when his wonderfully stable, well-regulated, but immobile world fell in ruin around him; and I am older than poor Daisy when she was driven out of the room thick in *Daily Mails* on the fourth floor of St Leonard's House. She remained as dirty as ever in her new lodgings, down a covered alley-way off Hythe Hill. But she soon became, so I was told, exceedingly unhappy. She died a very few years after her removal from her cluttered but safe upstairs place of familiarity with no great effort, slipping into death as easily as she had been in the habit of slipping into sleep. Indeed, I believe that she died *in* her sleep. I suppose Teddy Tail remained her guide and her companion to the very end. My father, who paid an allowance to her landlady, included in it an annual subscription to the *Daily Mail* for the rest of her life, which meant another 650 to 750 numbers. Indeed, Teddy Tail must have gone on coming for weeks, even months, after her death, seeking in vain his faithful companion of forty years or so.